Desert Fathers
and Mothers

Selected Books in the
SkyLight Illuminations Series

Desert Fathers and Mothers

Early Christian Wisdom Sayings—Annotated & Explained

Annotation by
Christine Valters Paintner, PhD

Walking Together, Finding the Way ®
SKYLIGHT PATHS®
PUBLISHING
Woodstock, Vermont

Desert Fathers and Mothers:
Early Christian Wisdom Sayings—Annotated & Explained
2016 Quality Paperback Edition, Second Printing

Grateful acknowledgment is given for permission to use excerpts from *Sayings of the Desert Fathers*, translated by Benedicta Ward, and originally published in English by Liturgical Press, Saint John's Abbey, Collegeville, Minnesota 56321, USA, and included in this edition by license of Liturgical Press. All rights reserved.

Annotation and introductory material © 2012 by Christine Valters Paintner

Library of Congress Cataloging-in-Publication Data

Paintner, Christine Valters.
  Desert fathers and mothers : early Christian wisdom sayings, annotated & explained / annotation by Christine Valters Paintner.
     p. cm. — (Skylight illuminations)
  Includes bibliographical references.
  ISBN 978-1-59473-373-4 (quality pbk.)
  1. Desert Fathers. 2. Desert Fathers—Quotations. 3. Spiritual life—Christianity—Quotations, maxims, etc. 4. Christian life—Quotations, maxims, etc. I. Title.
  BR67.P355 2012
  270.2—dc23
                              2012022524
ISBN 978-1-59473-470-0 (eBook)
10 9 8 7 6 5 4 3 2
Manufactured in the United States of America

Cover Design: Walter C. Bumford III, Stockton, Massachusetts, and Gloria Todt
Cover Art: © CharlesGibson/Bigstock.com

SkyLight Paths Publishing is creating a place where people of different spiritual traditions come together for challenge and inspiration, a place where we can help each other understand the mystery that lies at the heart of our existence.

SkyLight Paths sees both believers and seekers as a community that increasingly transcends traditional boundaries of religion and denomination—people wanting to learn from each other, *walking together, finding the way.*

SkyLight Paths, "Walking Together, Finding the Way" and colophon are trademarks of LongHill Partners, Inc., registered in the U.S. Patent and Trademark Office.

Walking Together, Finding the Way®

Published by SkyLight Paths® Publishing
A Division of LongHill Partners, Inc.
Sunset Farm Offices, Route 4, P.O. Box 237
Woodstock, VT 05091
Tel: (802) 457-4000   Fax: (802) 457-4004
www.skylightpaths.com

To my beautiful mother-in-law, Helen, who was a monk at heart. She entered the terrible desert of Alzheimer's that eventually ended her life in 2011. May she find her place singing among the angels and offering solace to desert pilgrims.

The road of cleansing goes through that desert. It shall be named the way of holiness.

—Isaiah 35:8

In the deserts of the heart, let the healing fountain start.
—W. H. Auden, "In Memory of W. B. Yeats"

For the garden is the only place there is,
but you will not find it
Until you have looked for it everywhere and found nowhere
that is not a desert.
—W. H. Auden, "For the Time Being"

If the desert is holy, it is because it is a forgotten place that allows us to remember the sacred. Perhaps that is why every pilgrimage to the desert is a pilgrimage to the self. There is no place to hide and so we are found.
—Terry Tempest Williams,
Refuge: An Unnatural History of Family and Place

Contents ▨

Introduction □

What is a monk?
A monk is someone who every day asks:
"What is a monk?"
—Cistercian monk Dom Andre Louf

In the third- to sixth-century desert landscape of Egypt, Syria, Palestine, and Arabia, a powerful movement was happening. Christian monasticism began flowering in response to a call to leave behind "the world." The center of this movement was in Egypt; by the year 400 CE Egypt was a land of monks experimenting with a variety of forms of monasticism including the solitary life of the hermit, the cenobitic or communal form of monasticism, and the gathering together of groups of ascetics living close to one another. These spiritual seekers, who came be known as the desert fathers and mothers, withdrew from a society where the misuse of human relationships, power, and material possessions ran counter to their sense of the sacredness of life.

Their journey into the desert was a movement toward cultivating an intentional awareness of God's presence and recognizing that worldly pleasures bring little long-term satisfaction. The aim was to experience God in each moment and activity by reducing their physical needs and committing themselves to the discipline of regular prayer and self-inquiry.

In this time and place, a literary genre emerged that was similar in form to parables and proverbs—teachings through story to impart wisdom. These were gathered together in a text called the *Sayings of the Desert Fathers* (*Apophthegmata Patrum*), which includes sayings from both the desert fathers and the desert mothers.

The Desert Mystique: Stripping Us Down to the Sacred Essentials

The word for "desert" in Greek is *eremos* and means "abandonment." It is the term from which we derive the word "hermit." The desert was a place to come face-to-face with loneliness and death. Nothing grows in the desert. Your very existence is, therefore, threatened. In the desert, you are forced to face up to yourself and to the temptations in life that distract you from a wide-hearted focus on the presence of the sacred in the world.

The desert is a place of deep encounter, not a place of superficial escape. It is a place that strips you down to the essentials, forcing you to let go of all the securities you cling to in life, even your images of God. The desert leaves you feeling alone, mortal, limited. Yet it is through the fierceness of this very experience that the desert elders saw a doorway to an encounter with a God who was much more expansive than anything believers imagined.

The wisdom of this tradition formed the foundation for much of the Christian spirituality that developed in the centuries that followed, especially Benedictine and Celtic forms of monasticism. In our current day, the lessons of the desert speak powerfully to us across almost two millennia, proof of their timeless wisdom. In an age when many are turning to the spirituality of eastern traditions, Christianity offers its own insights about meditation, dealing with thoughts and distractions, and cultivating attentive presence to each moment—insights that are similar to what we find in the beauty of Yogic or Buddhist practices.

The desert fathers and mothers were primarily concerned with what poet John Keats called the ancient task of "soul-making."[1] The only requirement of this task is to wake ourselves up and to remember who we really are. According to the desert tradition, we have forgotten our true worth and the source of that worth; we have fallen asleep to the true nature of life. We have numbed ourselves to the struggles of living. In the desert tradition, sin might be described as this act of forgetting the treasures we each carry simply by virtue of our divine inheritance.

Paula Huston, a Camaldolese oblate and writer on monastic spirituality, shared this observation about the role of sin in the spiritual life:

> Sin is complicated because it is rooted in lying. In order to convince ourselves to enter into sin, we must in some way deceive ourselves—rationalize away our doubts, tell ourselves a consoling story about our real motivations. Each lie necessitates another, and eventually we wind up morally and spiritually blind. Humility, on the other hand, refuses to self-justify. Humility would rather be unfairly accused than take the risk of egoistic self-deception. And thus it helps foster clarity of vision.[2]

The desert elders were especially alert to the ways we lie to ourselves and the mental chain of events that may lead us to rationalize our behaviors until we end up in a state of blindness.

They were concerned primarily with moving toward truth and love through the practices of humility and letting go. Alan Jones, former dean of Grace Cathedral in San Francisco, writes that those who are willing to take the journey into the desert have two main features: "a heart and mind willing to pursue the truth wherever it may lead (and the ability to acknowledge that they may be wrong); and the kind of sensibility (which is the joining of the mind and heart) that is captive to wonder, mystery, and awe."[3] The desert demands that we acknowledge the frail and limited places within ourselves. In embracing our imperfections, paradoxically, we are brought to a place of profound wonder at life and creation. When we desire to see ourselves and our motivations more clearly, we slowly begin to see God more clearly. The wisdom of the desert fathers and mothers has remained important in every age, because it is about the fundamental struggle to live a meaningful and authentic life. In current times, particularly, their wisdom offers a challenge to the values of our contemporary culture—values finely focused on productivity, achievement, "power over" rather than shared power, self-interest rather than interest in the common good, and self-preservation at all costs.

In many ways, the ethos of our times is similar to that which prompted the ancient monks to flee out into the desert. Many of us are similarly seeking ways of breaking free from the overwhelming demands of modern life and from a worldview focused so much on accumulation of material wealth, seeking ways of living with integrity and congruence between our inner convictions and our actions in the world. It takes courage and insight to live in active resistance to the destructive forces in the culture around us. Desert wisdom strengthens us by helping us to see that our relationship to God is at the center of our lives' meaning.

In his book on desert and mountain spirituality, *The Solace of Fierce Landscapes,* theologian Belden Lane writes, "Certain truths can be learned, it seems, only as one is sufficiently emptied, frightened, or confused." The desire to go out into the desert is a desire to be stripped bare of all pretension so that we might see what is real. He goes on to write:

> My fear is that much of what we call "spirituality" today is overly sanitized and sterile, far removed from the anguish of pain, the anchoredness of place. Without the tough-minded discipline of desert-mountain experience, spirituality loses its bite, its capacity to speak prophetically to its culture, its demand for justice. Avoiding pain and confrontation, it makes no demands, assumes no risks.... It resists every form of desert perversity, dissolving at last into a spirituality that protects its readers from the vulnerability it was meant to provoke. The desert, in the end, will have none of it.[4]

Desert spirituality is about allowing ourselves to be broken open and to meet our attachments with a fierce willingness to surrender them. The desert demands that we be vulnerable. This is no comforting path assuring us tritely that "everything happens for a reason"; the God of the desert elders shatters the boxes within which we try to confine the sacred.

We do not have to journey to the literal desert to encounter its power. Each of us has desert encounters—experiences that strip away all our comforts and assurances and leave us to face ourselves directly. When illness, death, or loss of any significance visits us, we are thrust into the landscape of the desert. Each of us can benefit from the wisdom of the desert fathers and mothers, who speak to us across time about the meaning and grace possible there. The symbolic, yet very human, dimension of life in the desert is common to us all.

The desert is not a place of personal retreat, but a place of spiritual revolution. It is:

> A desert of the spirit: a place of silence, waiting, and temptation. It is also the place of revelation, conversion, and transformation. A true revelation is a very disturbing event because it demands a response; and to respond to it means some kind of inner revolution. It involves being "made over," being made new, being "born again." The desert, then, is a place of revelation and revolution. In the desert we wait, we weep, we learn to live.[5]

The desert is a place of deep encounter, not of superficial escape. The ultimate paradox of the desert is that to find ourselves in it, we have to relinquish everything we think we know about ourselves.

Ultimately, and in contrast to the "sanitized and sterile" spirituality of today that Belden Lane warns against, desert monastics were fiercely uncompromising in their advice for fellow pilgrims traveling the interior geography of the human heart. This fierceness is refreshing; it takes our woundedness seriously but always points back to our beauty as creatures of God. As theologian John Chryssavgis puts it, "The desert produced healers, not thinkers."[6] Their wisdom is in the service of healing and love rather than theological systematization of ideas or doctrine.

St. Benedict (ca. 480–547), one of the key figures in the development of monasticism, was deeply influenced by the desert elders. Written by Benedict fifteen hundred years ago, his Rule wisely states, "Always we begin again."[7] While the desert often brings endings, it is also a place of new beginnings. The desert is a place to enter into the refiner's fire and be stripped down to one's holy essence. It is a threshold place where you emerge different than when you entered. It is where Jesus began his ministry. It is where each of us is called to begin our renewed path toward the Divine.

Scholar of religion Andrew Harvey once wrote, "The things that ignore us save us in the end. Their presence awakens silence in us; they refresh our courage with the purity of their detachment."[8] One of the goals of spiritual life in desert tradition was detachment from our desires and agendas. Being in the desert landscape reminds us of what that means on a visceral level. The harshness of that landscape helps to clarify the mind and reorder priorities. Surroundings that are not conditioned by our meek presence, which do not exist solely for us, are able to set us free. For a moment in time the world is not there to serve us; we fade into the background. We can release our frantic quest for self-fulfillment and return to what is deeply true and meaningful, to the essence of spiritual life.

The desert is ultimately a metaphor for inner attentiveness, vulnerability, and transformation. It is the still point within each of us where God and the true self dwell. Quoted in Kerry Walters's *Soul Wilderness*, Roman Catholic theologian Karl Rahner refers to "the call of the inner desert as divine grace, the hushed summons of divine mystery."[9] The starting place of the desert is our experience of being at risk.

Religious, Social, and Political Context of Third- and Fourth-Century Egypt

St. Anthony (ca. 251–256), also known as St. Anthony the Great, is considered to be the founder of the monastic movement. He moved into the desert at the end of the third century to seek solitude, and by the end of his life thousands had followed him there to imitate his extreme asceticism.

Paul of Thebes is actually recorded as the first monk in Christian tradition to live in the desert, but it was St. Anthony's example and story that ignited a movement. This was a period of great transition in the church. During the first and second centuries, to be Christian was illegal, and many were martyred for their faith. In 313 CE, Christianity became tolerated and, soon after, became the religion of an empire. People continued to flee to the desert to find a place where they could live a holy life free from the perversions of their culture. In his book *Listen to the Desert*, Father Gregory Mayers writes:

> When they began to wake from this shared trance, when they suspected they were more slaves than free, the men and women of the desert sayings fled their culture to escape the disguises and distractions it perpetrated on their human spirits. It is no small act of courage to face squarely the fictions in our life and the troubling sense that something isn't quite right about our life.[10]

Leaving behind the inhabited world became a new form of martyrdom. Those who had been killed under Roman persecution were part of what was known as the "red martyrdom." Once Christianity became legal, those who retreated to the desert were part of what was called "white martyrdom"—a movement in conscious resistance to the co-opting of Christian values as a way to hold up a power system.[11]

Those who went to the desert came from all walks of life—some had been living a wealthy life in the city, some had been poor farmers. Some had education; others had little. This coming together of disparate people and experiences for a common goal was a living example of what Christian community was supposed to be—no distinction between disciples. This diversity had a significant impact on the monastic tradition that followed. St. Benedict was careful to include principles in his Rule to help the monks in his community treat everyone as an equal.

David R. Keller writes in his book *Oasis of Wisdom* that the roots of Christian monasticism included three foundational "events," which we move through in order. First is *oikoumene*, which is an inner awareness that the inhabited world is a distraction from a deep personal longing to seek God and live out Gospel values and commitments. Second is *anachoresis*, which is the physical separation from society's values and our usual life patterns and relationships through a withdrawal into the desert. Third is *eremos*, the Greek word for "desert," which may be experienced as an internal event or external location. The desert is the place of separation from the world in service of complete dedication to and dependence on God.[12]

Those who dedicated themselves to the life of the desert sought out a spiritual elder. Their lives were centered on committing themselves to continual prayer, freeing themselves from the tyranny of thoughts, keeping their lives simple so as to focus on God, and memorizing scripture so they had sacred wisdom within easy access, as books were very rare at the time.

Patterns of Monasticism and Their Founders

The great center of the desert tradition was Egypt. There were three main patterns of monastic experiments that emerged in Egypt:

Hermit Life

St. Anthony the Great, who lived in lower Egypt, is considered the prototype of the hermit experience and is considered to be one of the founders of this way of life. One day while in church, he heard the command of Jesus: "If you wish to be perfect, go, sell your possessions, and give the money to the poor, and you will have treasure in heaven; then come, follow me" (Matthew 19:21), and he considered it addressed to himself directly. Thanks to *Life of Anthony* by Athanasius, we know more about Anthony than any of the other early ascetics.

Cenobitic Monasticism

St. Pachomius (290–347), who lived in Upper Egypt, became the creator of an organized form of monasticism and is considered to be the founder of its communal form. Communities of monks came together to unite with one another in work and prayer. This form is what gave rise to Christian monastic orders like the Benedictines and Augustinians.

Groups of Ascetics

In Nitria, west of the Nile Delta, and at Scetis, forty miles south of Nitria, there evolved another form of monastic life where several monks lived together, often as the disciples of an *abba*, or spiritual father. Those who gathered there tended to be more educated. Many of the famous desert fathers, such as Moses, Pambo, and Abraham, whose sayings appear in the text, came from this area.

A strong advocate for the monastic way of life and perhaps the most famous of the ascetics is Evagrius Ponticus (ca. 345–399). He was born in Asia Minor, was the student of St. Basil (the Greek Bishop of Caesarea) and St. Gregory Nazianzen (Archbishop of Constantinople), and later became a theologian in his own right. He eventually ended up in Egypt as a disciple of Abba Macarius—one of the desert fathers living in the Scetis desert—and began synthesizing their teachings. In his writing he describes the complementary nature of the practical life with the contemplative life in the desert way.

One of the main ambassadors for the monastic tradition in the West was John Cassian (ca. 360–435). He went to study monasticism in Egypt and was greatly influenced by Evagrius Ponticus; a monk and author of many treatises on desert wisdom. Cassian later formed two monasteries near Marseilles in France, where he wrote his *Institutes* and *Conferences*, which were presentations of what he had learned from the desert fathers. Cassian is quoted heavily in the Rule of Benedict and *Conferences* became one of the spiritual classics in the western Christian tradition. His attempts at systematization are his own and don't indicate any overall coherence in the desert texts.

Peasants who lived in the villages of Egypt along the Nile or in the Delta region considered the desert to be a place of terror. The boundaries of their lives in these village oases were created by desert landscape. The fertile land where the peasants lived was dedicated to Osiris, the god of life, and his son, Horus, and was posed against the god of the sterile desert, or the "red land" god, who was considered to be hostile and malevolent.[13] For the peasants, the desert was a place full of fear, a region of the dead, where bands of nomads who were hostile to outsiders and strangers lived. The desert was home to dangerous animals like snakes and jackals. In the *Life of Anthony*, the desert is described as a wilderness of beasts and demons.[14]

Being among the beasts did not frighten the desert elders. One characteristic that often distinguished a saint as different from others was their kinship with animals. Most often, the desert fathers and mothers were associated with the lion.[15] This was in part because the lion represented the Gospel According to Mark, which begins with the words of a voice crying out in the desert. In early Christianity, the lion symbolized resurrection. Believers were often thrown to the lions; many stories exist of the lions running up to these holy ones and falling before them in reverence, licking their feet. This reversal of codes and behavior indicated that the lion was able to sense or smell the holiness of a person. In the story of the death of Mary of Egypt, one of the desert mothers, the monk Zosimas, is too old to dig her grave, so a lion arrives, licks the feet of her body, and then digs the grave with his great paws.[16]

Those who fled into the desert seeking solitude and silence took the name "monk" for themselves. Derived from the Greek word *monachos,* "monk" means "solitary" or "single." The name referred not to their living status but instead to their focus. The desert provided a landscape in which they could release all distractions and bring their full attention to the spiritual path.

Slowly, over time, the desert became inhabited with so many monks that it became a city and was referred to as *desertum ciuitas* (the desert a city).[17] Thousands of people made their homes there, and it became a spiritual landscape for doing battle with inner demons, as Jesus did in his own sojourn in the desert. This gathering of monks in the desert led to the creation of communities of monks, or monasteries.

The barbarian and Islamic conquests of the fifth through seventh centuries would mark the end of the desert period; however, even before this time there was a movement toward living more and more in communal structures and monasteries. The hermit ideal did not die out completely. In medieval England, for example, there were many female anchoresses who lived solitary lives. Some monastic orders tried to integrate the hermit ideal with communal living, such as the Carthusian order, where monks live mainly in solitude but gather together for prayer three times each day.[18]

All these monks compose "the desert fathers and mothers," but especially those whose sayings are left to us in the *Apophthegmata Patrum*. These stories and wisdom were typically presented in the form of a conversation between a younger monk and his or her spiritual father or mother; they emerge from an oral tradition and are organized alphabetically by first name.

The wisdom of the desert has had a significant impact on the development of Christian spirituality, especially in the Benedictine and Celtic monastic traditions of the West and in the monasticism of Eastern Orthodox churches. I will be exploring some of these traditions in my commentary throughout this book.

Continued Development of Monastic Tradition

The desert tradition continued in the monasteries of the Coptic churches of Ethiopia and Egypt, as well as in the Greek Orthodox tradition; active monasteries are found to this day in places like Mount Athos in Greece and St. Catherine's Monastery below Mount Sinai in Egypt. They carry on the original ascetic practices of self-denial and living in harsh conditions as part of their spiritual path, and the wisdom of the desert elders continues to guide them.

As mentioned earlier, people like John Cassian brought monasticism to Western Europe and helped it flower there. The first people in Europe to take on the life of the hermits were the Celtic Christians in Gaul in the early fourth century. The Celts carried this tradition to Ireland where monasticism contributed to the spread of Christianity.

Rather than living in the harsh heat of the desert, Celtic monastics submitted themselves to life in the cold wilderness, often settling in hard-to-reach places. Through the efforts of people like St. Patrick, Christianity slowly grew as a presence until the sixth century when many of the great Irish monasteries were founded and the monks moved from small clusters of hermit cells to more established centers of power.

There are many stories of charismatic Irish leaders who spread the gift of monasticism through Ireland and Scotland, as well as in places like Lindisfarne, known as Holy Island, off the coast of Northumberland.

Around the same time, in the early sixth century, St. Benedict founded his first monasteries in Subiaco, Italy, near the cave where he retreated as a hermit for three years. He attracted many disciples and, with them, he established twelve monasteries, each composed of twelve monks. Later in his life he also established a monastery in Monte Cassino. Benedict's Rule, which became the basis of the Benedictine order, was written for his monks at Monte Cassino.

In writing his Rule, Benedict made use of several earlier monastic teachings, such as the Rule of Augustine and the Rule of the Master. Benedict's Rule spread through Roman Catholic Europe primarily because of its clarity and commitment to moderation in all things, and so, in this sense, differs from the more strict ascetic traditions of Egypt or Ireland. In Benedict's Rule, there is more of an emphasis on a balanced life.

Gender and the Desert

While the Latin name of the core desert wisdom text is *Apophthegmata Patrum*, with a strict translation of *Sayings of the Desert Fathers*, several sayings of desert mothers are also included. There is a small collection of female desert elders' sayings found in other sources, as well.

Generally, women in the early Christian centuries did not own themselves; they did not have control of their lives or even their bodies. Women were at the disposal of other people, generally men, who owned them.

In the desert, however, women were able to reject these constraints and restrictions. In the desert, the *ammas* (mothers) were able to live with the same single focus as the *abbas* (fathers)—growing in intimacy with the divine presence. These women were as fierce in their spiritual wisdom as their male counterparts. The titles "spiritual father" and "spiritual mother" were given not because the individuals played any kind of nurturing role, but because they were considered to be wise elders steeped in years of desert experience.

When these women decided to leave their conventional lives behind—many of them were well educated, some were quite wealthy, some were prostitutes—they each made an intentional choice to live in a way different from that of the dominant culture. The history of the *ammas* reveals that, from the very beginnings of the life of the church, women have been initiators of new patterns and teachings.

Both men and women were considered to be *pneumataphores*, or "bearers of the spirit." Mary Forman, in her book on desert mothers, explored the meaning of this term as used in the early Christian east and found that it referred to those who were spiritual, inspired, and prophetic, both men and women.[19]

Unfortunately, we don't know as much about the desert mothers as we do about their male counterparts, and the sayings of the desert fathers far outnumber those of the mothers. Yet there are several desert mothers who lived in communities of their own. Amma Syncletica is one of the best-known of these women, and she was taken very seriously by the male tradition. In the fourth century, Gregory of Nyssa wrote about the life of his sister, St. Macrina, and in it he refers to Amma Syncletica throughout as "the teacher."

Thankfully, we have some supplemental texts now available to help flesh out this tradition in greater detail. These include Laura Swan's *The Forgotten Desert Mothers: Sayings, Lives, and Stories of Early Christian Women* and Mary Forman's *The Desert Mothers: Spiritual Practices from the Women of the Wilderness*.

We might look at one story from the tradition of the desert mothers to get a sense of what was at play in this culture:

Another time, two old men, great anchorites, came to the district of Pelusia to visit her. When they arrived one said to the other, "Let us humiliate this old woman." So they said to her, "Be careful not to become conceited in thinking to yourself: 'Look how anchorites are coming to see me, a mere woman.'" But Amma Sarah said

> to them, "According to nature I am a woman, but not according to my thoughts."
>
> —Sarah 4

According to Mary Forman, this kind of clever wordplay was common in Amma Sarah's time. She recognizes that physically she is a woman, but spiritually her identity is much larger than this. In a patriarchal culture, it was up to women to prove their strength in the spiritual life, to act more "manly" as it were. There were many women revered and honored for their spiritual wisdom and strength. We know women were a very active presence in the desert.[20]

There are many points in the *Sayings of the Desert Fathers* where the monks warn the young disciples to avoid being in the presence of women. The premise is that those who were new to the desert had not yet matured enough in the interior life to manage their sexual fantasies or conduct themselves appropriately.

> There is a story which describes a monk who "was once bitten by a snake, and went to a certain city to be cured. He was received by a pious and God-fearing woman, and she healed him. When the pain had subsided a bit, the devil began to suggest things to him, and he wanted to touch the woman's hand. She said to him, 'Do not do this, father, have regard for Christ. Think of the grief and contrition you will experience when you are in your cell. Think of the groans and tears which will be yours.' When he heard these and similar things from her, the attack left him and he was greatly embarrassed, wanting to flee because he could not look her in the eye. She, with the mercy of Christ, said to him, 'Do not be ashamed that you still have progress to make. Those things did not come from your own pure soul, but the suggestion was made through the devil's wickedness.' Thus she healed him without scandal and sent him on his way with provisions for the journey."[21]

This story offers a refreshing window into desert life, because it is the woman who is the instrument of grace and compassion, rather than purely the object of temptation. She knew the monk was a good person; she extended great kindness by accepting his faults and hospitality by providing him what he needed.

As monastic communities spread and flourished in places across Europe and the British Isles, women were consistently present in large numbers as well, forming their own monasteries and living the committed life alongside of men.

Significant Figures

With one hundred thirty voices present in the *Sayings of the Desert Fathers*, there are a few who are especially significant by virtue of the amount of sayings attributed to them, their renown, or being one of the three women represented in the text.

Abba Anthony

We have already briefly explored the role that St. Anthony plays and his significance to the desert tradition. Athanasius of Alexandria, who wrote the aforementioned hagiography about St. Anthony that helped spread the story of his life, noted that even though he was not the first monk to go out into the desert, Anthony is considered to be the founder of the desert movement. Athanasius's *Life of Anthony* describes the multitude of demons with which he did courageous battle and which have been depicted in many works of art. St. Anthony has thirty-eight sayings attributed to him.

Abba Arsenius

The *Sayings of the Desert Fathers* tell us that Arsenius—also known as Arsenius the Great—left behind much wealth and comfort. Born in Rome around the year 354, he was well educated and was appointed by the emperor as a tutor to two princes. Arsenius left for the desert life at the age of forty and, once there, sought a life of strict solitude. He was known for his austerity and commitment to silence. There are forty-four sayings under his name.

Abba Poemen

Poemen is called "the quintessential Desert Father."[22] Having died around the year 449, he would have known other monks like John the Dwarf, Agathon, and Moses. He is known especially for his attention to monastic virtues and his emphasis on the congruence of the inner life and outer action in spiritual life. Almost 209 of the sayings are attributed to him, although there may have been more than one elder with his name.

Abba Macarius of Egypt

Macarius the Great was born around the year 300 in Egypt and died in 390. His first professions were as a camel-driver and a trader of goods; later he was an ordained priest. He is known for his humility, for acknowledging his limitations, and for his love and acceptance. Forty-one sayings appear under his name.

Abba Moses the Robber

Moses, a slave who had been freed, was known as a murderer and a robber in Nitria, Egypt. He became a monk later in his life and was a disciple of Isidore the Priest. There is a story about Moses tying up four robbers who entered his home after he became a monk. He brought them to church, and they all became monks themselves. He has seven sayings attributed to him.

Amma Syncletica

Syncletica is one of the three women who appear in the *Sayings of the Desert Fathers*. She was born to a wealthy family in Alexandria in the year 380. She was very well educated. When her parents died she sold everything, gave the earnings to the poor, and went with her blind sister to live as a hermit. Eventually, a community of women formed around her. She died in the year 460. She saw no distinction between monks who lived in the desert and monks who lived in the city—the spiritual call for both was the same. She felt that too many people were dwelling in the desert but still acting like they lived in the city. We have twenty-seven of her sayings in the collection.

Amma Sarah

Sarah came from Upper Egypt and was also a well-educated woman born into a wealthy family. She died around the age of eighty. Sarah is known for her focus on purity of heart and working to curb thoughts that might distract her from God. It is said that she lived over sixty years as a hermit by a river, but never lifted her eyes to look at it. She has nine sayings under her name.

Amma Theodora

Theodora lived in fourth-century Egypt, but little is known about her. She was what we, today, might call a spiritual director to bishops and other men in public position. She was one of the first desert elders to give a description of *acedia*, also called *accidie*, which refers to lack of initiative in spiritual practice. There are ten sayings attributed to her.

A Word about the Translation

The translation I use of the *Sayings of the Desert Fathers* is by Sister Benedicta Ward, OSB. This version is the only English translation of the most complete version of the *Apophthegmata Patrum* and is one of the most referenced translations in desert literature. It is known as the "alphabetical collection" because the sayings are presented in order by first name. Ward's translation reflects the language of the desert fathers and mothers—and the time they lived in—and as a result does not necessarily achieve the gender inclusiveness that we aim for today. I have left this translation as is to preserve its authenticity and it is my hope that all readers will find their way through to the desert sages' universal and timeless wisdom.

I did not limit myself only to the most significant of desert fathers and mothers mentioned above, but tried to include a diversity of voices in this book, including some from whom there are only one or two sayings. With about 1,200 sayings in all, from 127 fathers and three mothers,[23] my study is a small selection. I tried to include sayings that provided a variety of perspectives—desert wisdom is not a unified or codified approach to spiritual life, but instead is a diverse collection of reflections from many voices. And finally, I tried to address a number of different themes from the desert tradition, and chose stories that I felt best illuminated each theme chosen.

The *Apophthegmata Patrum*, or *Sayings of the Desert Fathers*, is not the only collection we have of desert wisdom. I also draw on a few other sources in addition to this translation, including the works of Evagrius Ponticus, John Cassian, and St. Benedict; John Chryssavgis's translations of the *Reflections of Zosimas*; stories from an Anonymous series of sayings;[24] and the *Verba Seniorum*[25] (stories of the elders from a Latin translation of the Greek original, many of which can be found in an English translation by Thomas Merton).

In the translator's note for the *Sayings of the Desert Fathers*, Sister Benedicta Ward writes that the text presents challenges because it developed first in oral form and was only later documented in written form. The initial stage of transmission of these sayings was oral and was in the Coptic, Syriac, Greek, and Latin languages. The sayings were the spontaneous responses of wise elders to the concerns of those disciples who traveled to see them. The next stage of transmission happened toward the end of the fourth and in the early fifth centuries when the sayings were written down; they lost some of their freshness and directness as they were recorded and codified. In the middle of the fifth century, these original texts were then edited into several collections, of which the *Apophthegmata Patrum* is one. Finally, over 1,500 years went by before we, as modern readers, approached them in their translated form.

Chryssavgis's *Reflections* describes the effect that reading the sayings has on Abba Zosimas:

> The blessed Zosimas always loved to read these Sayings of the Holy Fathers all the time; they were almost like the air that he breathed. It is from these Sayings that he came to receive the fruit of every virtue.[26]

Despite our distance from the original stories in terms of both time and culture, the sayings are able to offer us this same richness, fruit, and life-giving breath of air.

Desert Themes, Key Terms, and Organizational Structure

Sayings of the Desert Fathers launched a new literary genre in its time, closer to parables and folk wisdom in nature. The sayings preserve the wisdom of the desert monastic tradition in an unstructured way, different from John Cassian's works, which attempt to systematize monastic understanding. The fathers and mothers of the desert did not have a systematic way of life; they had only the hard work of attempting to focus the body, mind, and soul back toward God at every turn. Since they reflect the voices of individuals, the sayings are not always consistent; they are a record of practical wisdom that emerged out of many lives of experience.

Yet when we read the texts together, many dominant ideas emerge. In the original text of *Sayings of the Desert Fathers*, the sayings are organized alphabetically by first name according to who said them, so that all the sayings of Abba Anthony are grouped together and so on. The effect of this feels organic; it works well to give the reader a sense of the different monks' perspectives. However, for the sake of drawing comparisons and connecting subjects between monks, this book—like most commentaries on the desert tradition—is organized according to themes. Within each theme, several sayings are grouped from different desert elders. This allows us to explore how a particular idea was expressed through different elders and to appreciate both the similarities and differences in their approaches.

I chose the themes based on what I felt were most significant to an essential understanding of the desert way of spirituality. I begin with reflections on the common phrase "Give me a word," as well as on the importance of the two foundational ideas in desert spirituality, the cell and the heart, where the hard work of transformation takes place. Then I explore the roles of thoughts, desires, and passions. For the monk, his or her daily practice was to be aware and attentive to what the mind was doing and to transform any obsessions within it. This was cultivated through the next themes: first, the virtue of humility—a radical letting go of things as well as ideas, and then through the act of embracing the heart of a beginner in the spiritual life. I then examine the essential nature of the wise elder with whom one could share the temptations and struggles of life.

According to the desert fathers and mothers, the longer we practice and work to heal our places of wounding, the more we will encounter the rising up of the "gift of tears." These tears are signs of both our sorrow over how we have rejected our true nature and our joy in our discovery of the beauty of God. Practice is at the heart of this work, with a focus on showing up each day. The spiritual life for the elders cultivated the capacity for greater and greater love, service to others, and a more profound sense of inner stillness. I end with a consideration of the multiplicity of voices and insights the desert monks offer to us and finally, how to become a monk ourselves.

Among the themes examined are several Greek terms the desert elders used in specific ways, such as: *acedia*, which refers to a kind of restlessness in the spiritual life; the patience of *hupomone*; the watchfulness of *nepsis*; and the profound inner silence of *hesychia*, which is the ultimate goal of the spiritual life. As in all translations, the definitions are more slippery than they appear, but hopefully in reading the sayings themselves and reflecting on your own experiences, you will gain a deeper appreciation for the nuances and subtleties of the spiritual life they explore.

Each chapter is focused on one of the themes and includes several examples of sayings that illuminate its meaning. Along with these sayings I offer commentary, both on the meanings of the words as well as the invitations offered to us by these voices.

God of the Desert

The desert journey isn't about embarking on a long and arduous struggle to find God at the end of the road. Desert spirituality is about looking for

God right in the very midst of wrestling with ourselves. God is in the heart of the struggle, and so we are to stay there with the holy presence until the treasure is revealed.

The desert fathers and mothers believed that God is always with us, never absent, even when in the struggle we experience a kind of absence or loss of our comfortable understanding of who God is and how God works in the world. God loves us and stays with us no matter who we are or what we are doing. We are loved in the middle of life's messiness, in the wounded places.

Within this utter humility and surrender, where we encounter the Divine and discover this infinite love embracing us, even in the midst of brokenness, we also discover how to love others. As we come to accept our own limitations, we begin to accept the limitations of others with more grace and compassion.

Some of us may ask whether the inward journey of the desert is selfish in the face of so much suffering in the world. Is the path of the monk or hermit a path of fleeing our responsibility to others? For those in the desert, the practice of hospitality became indispensable. The contemplative life is meant to cultivate our ability to open our hearts to the stranger we encounter both in our outer worlds as well as within.

When we use service as an excuse to avoid the hard work of transformation, our love becomes more restricted and is slowly depleted. Working to heal the world can become its own form of numbing and avoiding our own inner wounds. A paradox of the spiritual life is that the more we enter our hearts, the more we are called back to love the world and offer a spacious compassion to others.

My Background

I fell in love with the monastic tradition while in graduate school. I was studying for the History of Christian Spirituality exam, which covers two thousand years of practice, and the Benedictines in particular kept speaking to my heart through their commitment to balance and seeing the sacred in all things.

I later became a Benedictine oblate with St. Placid Priory in Lacey, Washington, and have developed my work through my website www.AbbeyoftheArts.com, an online community offering resources and classes in contemplative practice and creative expression. Much of my work focuses on becoming what Brother Wayne Teasdale first called a "monk in the world."[27] Anyone can live like a monk in their daily life, even if they are far from a monastery, are married, or have children. Being a monk in the world means cultivating a commitment to slowness, spaciousness, and attentiveness to the sacred dimension of each object and activity. The desert is a metaphor for an inner quality of awareness.

The deeper I entered into the Benedictine way of life and monastic spirituality, the more I was drawn toward the roots of this tradition, which is the desert wisdom. The desert fathers and mothers have been profound teachers for me on this path. While they fled to the solitude of the desert landscape, I find the desert in the midst of the city, and in the center of my heart. The desert is an archetypal experience, one that transcends geography and physical location. Therefore, their teachings on how to become fully present to our inner thoughts and how to cultivate a deep peace apply whether in a rural or urban environment.

The older I get, the more I encounter desert experiences in my life. I seek out the wisdom of the desert fathers and mothers—for courage in staying with my difficult experiences and for hope that these difficult journeys have a bigger purpose. I live the desert way in my ordinary life by making space for silence and solitude, staying present to my experiences, and seeking out elders and wise mentors.

Even as I wrote this book I encountered desert times in my life. My mother-in-law, Helen, who had struggled with Alzheimer's for several years, finally entered her last days. There was much relief in her letting go, but also great grief. Her husband did not want his beloved of almost fifty years to leave her body even though she had departed her mind long before; he was left bereft.

As I sat with her in those last few days of her life, I was aware how much this disease had taken from this once beautiful and vibrant woman. I felt wave after wave of grief rise up over how senseless the situation felt. And there, the desert elders met me in my grief, calling me to not look away, to stay with my experience, to stay with Helen even as she lay dying. The desert fathers and mothers don't offer up neat and tidy answers for life's struggles. They simply acknowledge that the struggles exist, often mysteriously in the place of our deepest encounters with God. The desert elders embrace mystery and unknowing. The desert strips away all trite and easy explanations for how the world works.

One of the reasons I love Belden Lane's book on desert spirituality so much is because he weaves his research with narrative about his own mother's slow dying. He sees the nursing home and the hospital as a contemporary place of the desert experience. He asks, "What can be said of God that may be spoken without shame in the presence of those who are dying?"[28]

As I wrote this manuscript I was also preparing to embark on a grand adventure and live overseas with my husband for a year or longer. We sold almost everything we owned to free ourselves for this journey. And while this was a voluntary letting go, it was still difficult to leave behind all the comforts of my former life. There is always sacrifice in responding to a call and I felt the desert elders whispering their support. Their wisdom was very present to me as I listened for what to release so that I was able to be more free to respond to this holy direction.

I have also been drawn to yoga philosophy over the last fifteen years. I began, like many Westerners, with the physical practice of *asanas* or poses, but over time was drawn more to the philosophical roots. What I have discovered is that much of what the yoga sutras teach is congruent with the teachings of the desert fathers and mothers. It is a gift to reflect on these teachings in light of my own practice and find support there as well. There is a universality to the teachings of the desert, a wisdom that we find across traditions among those who practice a contemplative way of life.

How to Approach the Sayings

> *You stand outside the door, reading one more book about*
> *how to open the door. You note in your journal one more*
> *thought about what it might be like. Yet the longings of*
> *your heart remain.... Let today be the day you open the*
> *door of your heart to God.*
>
> —Joyce Rupp, *Open the Door: A Journey to the True Self*

This book is meant as an introduction to the wisdom of these wise elders, to make their thought and practice more accessible in our times. Rather than simply reading a book about how to open the door, as Joyce Rupp provocatively writes, the desert *abbas* and *ammas* invite you to actually open the door yourself and experience what that is like.

This book invites you to explore and engage with the insights and wisdom of the fathers and mothers who went to the desert to live out a simple but challenging spirituality that still resonates strongly with us today. In the process, you may take your own pilgrimage to the desert and journey to your own deepest self.

This is not a book to sit down and read cover to cover. You could certainly approach it in this way and gain an intellectual understanding of the concepts I explore. But the wisdom sayings of the desert fathers and mothers are more like Zen koans, texts to be pondered and chewed on slowly and then integrated into your life.

A more effective approach is to allow some time each day to read one section at a time twice through slowly. When a saying especially catches your attention, consider pausing and engaging with it through a form of prayer called *lectio divina*, which means sacred reading.

The ancient practice of *lectio divina*,[29] which emerged from the desert monks, is a practice of reading a sacred text slowly, listening for a word that is calling to your heart, then savoring the images that emerge in response, followed by tending to the invitation being offered. *Lectio divina* is a cyclical prayer; we return again and again to the words we want to integrate into our way of being in the world, and we allow them to work on us as we work on them.

You might also consider memorizing certain lines that captivate you, learning them by heart. Since the desert elders couldn't take books into the desert, they memorized scripture in order to always have it with them.

As you read the stories, it can also help to keep a journal and make notes of words and phrases that feel significant to you. Let this be a space to engage with what the desert elders are teaching. See if it rings true for your own experience. Allow time to read and then reflect and ponder.

Finally, you might purchase a copy of Benedicta Ward's translation of the *Sayings of the Desert Fathers* so that you have the original text, with many more sayings than I could include in this space. There is also a resource section at the end of this book to explore further.

The more you sit with these sayings and allow them to be integrated into your life and practice, the more layers of wisdom will be revealed. I have been praying with the texts of the desert for several years and still feel very much like a beginner on the spiritual path.

In the foreword to *Sayings of the Desert Fathers*, Anthony of Sourozh writes:

> If we wish to understand the sayings of the Fathers, let us approach
> them with veneration, silencing our judgments and our own thoughts
> in order to meet them on their own ground and perhaps to partake
> ultimately … in their own silent communion with God.[30]

I invite you to meet the desert elders on their terms. Remember that their culture and time were very different from ours, and so when we hear things that are challenging, rather than reject them outright, we can sit with them and see if there are any kernels of truth for us speaking across time and space.

The challenge in writing a book like this is the illusion of system-atization by placing sayings according to categories. This placement can help our minds to see patterns, but then we are lured into the danger of thinking of this as a "ten-step program for transformation." The wisdom of the desert is intuitive rather than analytic, spiral rather than linear. We circle around a variety of ideas, each of which is interconnected. Even to know where to begin writing and how to move through the book becomes challenging, because as I bring up one concept it inevitably touches on something else. As you read, if something feels unclear, see if you can rest in the discomfort of that place of unknowing. Later in the text you may come across more wisdom that illumines the points further.

Finally, remember that what you read here is only a fraction of the materials and texts available to us. I do not pretend to offer an exhaustive summary, and in my selectivity I will necessarily have missed some other important themes. But my hope is that there is just enough here to develop an appreciation for the profound wisdom these ancient men and women have to offer us.

Acknowledgments

As with any book, there is a whole community of support that goes into bringing it to fruition. I want to express heartfelt gratitude to:

My beloved husband John;

To the students in my classes who helped me to refine my ideas and make them even more accessible to a contemporary audience;

To the fine editors at SkyLight Paths, Emily Wichland, vice president of Editorial and Production, and Justine Earnest, assistant editor, for all the ways they helped bring this book to print;

To my Benedictine community of Sisters of St. Placid Priory and fellow oblates.

I am also grateful for the many desert experiences of my own life and the ways they have deepened my compassion.

I am profoundly grateful for the courageous men and women who journeyed to their own frontier thousands of years ago and for those who set their stories down in writing.

Desert Fathers
and Mothers

1 This is a key phrase, repeated often in the *Sayings of the Desert Fathers*. When a novice approaches one of the *ammas* or *abbas* and says "Give me a word," "he or she is not asking for either a command or a solution, but for a communication that can be received as a stimulus to grow into fuller life. It is never a theoretical matter, and the elders are scathing about those who want simply something to discuss" (Rowan Williams, *Silence and Honey Cakes: The Wisdom of the Desert* [Lion, 2003], 50).

This tradition of asking for a word was a way of seeking something on which to ponder for many days, weeks, months, sometimes even a whole lifetime. The word was often a short phrase to nourish and challenge the receiver. The word was meant to be wrestled with and slowly grown into.

2 For an explanation of "cell," see chapter 2, note 1.

☐ Give Me a Word

A brother questioned Abba Hierax saying, "Give me a word.[1] How can I be saved?" The old man said to him, "Sit in your cell,[2] and if you are hungry, eat; if you are thirsty, drink; only do not speaxk evil of anyone, and you will be saved."

(HIERAX 1)

 3 For an explanation of "cell," see chapter 2, note 1.

 4 This story demonstrates how a word could be worked on for years at a time. The word being sought was not a theological explanation or counseling. It was part of a relationship that had developed between elder and novice and the assumption was that this word, when received by the disciple, would be life-giving. This word, highly contextual and spoken with simplicity and directness, was meant for this person in this moment of their lives.

 5 This excerpt is drawn from Benedicta Ward, *Sayings of the Desert Fathers*, p. xxii. She does not include the attribution for this story.

 ✳ As you work through the wisdom of the desert fathers and mothers, consider releasing your thinking mind and enter into a space of receiving. Imagine yourself in the story and ask for your own life-giving word. The word might be an insight from the text. It might come in that time of stillness or it might arrive later in the day in the form of a line of poetry, wisdom offered from an unexpected source, a dream symbol, or an image you stumble upon that seizes your imagination.

 I often ask for a word as I take my daily walks. I listen for what the trees and pigeons might have to offer me. When I receive a word, often it is confirmed through synchronicities that continue to appear to me.

 The purpose of the word is to simply hold it in your heart, turning it over and over, pondering, but not analyzing it. Give it space within you to speak.

A monk once came to Basil of Caesarea and said, "Speak a word, Father"; and Basil replied, "Thou shalt love the Lord thy God with all thy heart," and the monk went away at once. Twenty years later he came back and said, "Father, I have struggled to keep your word; now speak another word to me"; and he said, "Thou shalt love thy neighbor as thyself"; and the monk returned in obedience to his cell[3] to keep that also.[4,5]

1 The desert fathers and mothers each lived alone in a simple hut or room called the "cell." In Benedictine monasteries, monks continue to live in these cells within the larger community, somewhat like a dormitory, and gather together in communal spaces for prayer and meals. In Celtic monasticism, we find gatherings of individual free-standing beehive huts, which functioned as the monks' cells, as well as an oratory, which was the place for the monks to come together for prayer and reading scripture.

This was the foundation for their spiritual journey. In the cell, you simply stay with yourself; you sit with your emotions; and you shut the door to any intrusion. This happens both literally and spiritually.

The monastic cell is a central concept in the spirituality of the desert fathers and mothers. This outer cell, which is the room where the monk lives, is a metaphor for the inner cell, a symbol of the deep soul work we are called to do to become fully awake. It is the place where we come into full presence with ourselves and all our inner voices, emotions, and challenges, where we strive to not abandon this soul work through distraction or numbing. It is also the place where we encounter God deep in our hearts.

If we can't find God right here, in this space, then we will not find God by going anywhere else. To "sit in your cell" means, on the surface, to close yourself in a space bordered by four walls and a ceiling. However, this is a voluntary confinement, not an act of self-punishment or penance. It is a way to retreat from the noise and activity of life and remove the disorienting and distracting voices—our own inner voices and those of others. In his book *Listen to the Desert*, Gregory Mayers describes it this way:

> Abba Moses' "cell" is a metaphor for the imprisoned self. If our appetite for the truth is strong enough to shore up our crumbling courage battered by the relentless onslaught of life's experiences, then we are rewarded by the emergence of the essence behind what is considered our self.... There is a final sense to the word

(continued on page 8)

☐ Your Cell Will Teach You Everything

A brother came to Scetis to visit Abba Moses and asked him for a word. The old man said to him: "Go sit in your cell,[1] and your cell will teach you everything."

(MOSES 6)

> "cell," meaning "the liberated self," wherein life becomes transparent and obvious.... "Your cell" has no walls, neither physical ones of mortar or wood, nor walls of flesh and bone, nor psychological ones defining a separate, independent self. The marketplace is your cell. (p. 7)

Abba Moses's advice points to something even deeper, a more interior journey. "Cell" means "self" as well. Sit with yourself and learn every detail of that inner landscape. Imagine sitting in a room for days on end—the way you would come to know the particular scents in the air, the way the light moves through the window, the knots in the floorboards, the chips in the paint. This is the kind of attention to our inner life that Abba Moses invites us to experience.

The more we cultivate this kind of awareness of our thoughts, emotions, and impulses, the more we learn that they come and they go; they rise and fall in intensity. Beneath all the tumultuousness of our inner life is a profound and deep pool of stillness from which we can behold this inner drama, yet not get lured into reacting to it. We develop an inner freedom and begin to discover something of the foundation of who we are that endures no matter the constantly shifting tides around us.

2 The Greek word *nepsis* means "watchfulness." It refers to a kind of calm vigilance in daily life, staying attentive and aware to the inner movements of the heart, watching one's thoughts, and noticing the patterns that arise. This inner attention, conducted with compassion, is the grace of the desert way.

Just as fish die if they stay too long out of water, so the monks who loiter outside their cell or pass their time with men of the world lose the intensity of inner peace. So like a fish going toward the sea, we must hurry to reach our cell, for fear that if we delay outside we shall lose our interior watchfulness.[2]

(ANTHONY 10)

✳ In 2011 I flew to Vienna, Austria, for a retreat. A few days after I landed, I developed symptoms of a blood clot and went to the emergency room. I was examined by the doctor, who told me there were several tests they needed to run. I was to stay in a wheelchair and not move about at all, because the clot could move to my heart or brain and cause instant death.

For eight hours my wheelchair became my monastic cell, the place where I practiced full presence to my inner life as best as I could. I witnessed my mind move between different states: terror that I could die at any moment, curiosity about how I felt about the possibility of dying sooner than I expected, awareness of my internal responses to getting test results, and, of course, distraction as a way of avoiding the whole process.

It ended up being a profound experience for me, and I was so grateful for having monastic wisdom and contemplative practice to carry me through those dark moments. I am also profoundly grateful to be alive. My practice of inner attention in daily life served me well in this time of stress and struggle, allowing me to stay awake to my experience rather than running away in my mind.

3 The desert fathers and mothers invite us to practice this kind of interior watchfulness, where we witness what happens inside our minds and hearts with compassion and commitment. Watchfulness is the antithesis of our ways of numbing ourselves to life, whether through watching hours of television, surfing the Internet, shopping, eating, or drinking. Anything can serve as a way of numbing ourselves when we engage in it as a way of avoiding what we are experiencing within. The desert fathers and mothers call us to become more conscious of the ways we avoid staying within our experiences.

Abba John gave this advice, "Watching means to sit in the cell³ and be always mindful of God. This is what is meant by, 'I was on watch and God came to me.'" (Matt. 25, 36)

(JOHN THE DWARF 27)

Amma Syncletica said, "There are many who live in the mountains and behave as if they were in town, and they are wasting their time. It is possible to be a solitary in one's mind while living in a crowd, and it is possible for one who is a solitary to live in the crowd of his own thoughts."

(SYNCLETICA 19)

✳   I live in the heart of the city and my monastic cell is a small apartment that I share with my husband. I love to go away on retreat, especially by the sea, but I would be fooling myself if I believed that living by the sea all the time would necessarily foster more inner silence. We may be tempted to think that those who live in monasteries have the advantage over those of us living "in the world." We might even begin to dismiss our own capacity or desire for silence, because it feels so difficult to achieve in the midst of city life.

I love being an urban monk precisely because I know that being a contemplative is not dependent upon location. While times of retreat are essential as ways to return us deeply to ourselves, ultimately it is in our daily lives that we discover the deep stillness offered to us. We carry our cell with us wherever we go. It is an interior quality of presence to our own experience.

Most of us have probably had the experience of sitting down to meditate and finding our minds noisy with chatter, never seeming to rest. Equally so, we have likely had moments in the midst of life's frenzied pace when suddenly we are overcome by a deep inner still-ness and peace about things. It may have been the way the light was reflecting off a loved one's face or remembering to take a deep breath that called us back to ourselves.

4   Connected to the cell is the cultivation of patience or steadfastness. The Greek word is *hupomone*, which essentially encourages us to stay with whatever is happening—just sit there and simply stay put. This means not running away physically or emotionally from ourselves, our passions, or our personal demons through our desire for distraction and relief.

This is similar to the central Benedictine concept of stability, which developed from the concept of *hupomone*. On one level, stability calls monks to a lifetime commitment within a particular community. St. Benedict required his monks to commit to a monastery for their entire lives so that they would be encouraged not to run away when things

(*continued on page 14*)

Someone said to Abba Arsenius "my thoughts trouble me, saying, 'You can neither fast nor work; at least go and visit the sick, for that is also charity.'" But the old man recognizing the suggestions of the demons, said to him, "Go, eat, drink, sleep, do no work; only do not leave your cell." For he knew that steadfastness in the cell⁴ keeps a monk in the right way.

(ARSENIUS 11)

got challenging. In his Rule, Benedict wrote, "from this day [of his monastic vows] he is no longer free to leave the monastery, nor to shake from his neck the yoke of the rule which, in the course of so prolonged a period of reflection, he was free to either reject or accept" (58:15).

On another level, the call is to not run away from conflict or difficulty in the midst of our lives. Stability and steadfastness demand that we stay with difficult experiences and stay present to the discomfort they create in us. Other desert sayings invite us to consider; however, that staying in one place for our lives does not guarantee that we will also be committed to an internal staying with our experience. Within the cell we will encounter boredom and loneliness. Our thoughts will begin to distract us and take us away from our experience.

5 Stability and patience call us to stay with our experience, to be fully present to whatever is happening within us. Moving about from place to place can be a form of distraction, redirecting our energies outside of us. If the cell represents the place where we encounter God, patience speaks to the time within which our encounter will happen. God's time is different than ours and the work of the cell is slow.

✳ We can experience the negative effects of jumping from place to place in our minds, as well. Even when the body is still, we let our minds carry us far back into the past or into the future. My own inclination is to live in the future, to always be planning ahead. My organized self loves calendars and to-do lists. These are important aspects of my work, but they can also become a way of avoiding my own experience in this moment, right now. I find myself sometimes so focused on checking things off my list that I miss the experience of the present moment.

[Amma Syncletica] also said, "If you find yourself in a monastery do not go to another place, for that will harm you a great deal.[5] Just as the bird who abandons the eggs she was sitting on prevents them from hatching, so the monk or the nun grows cold and their faith dies when they go from one place to another."

(SYNCLETICA 6)

6 We may be tempted to think that this emphasis on the monk's cell is a call to stay in solitude and silence, that somehow the spiritual life is more exalted in isolation. Or we may find relief in the impetus to sit in our cell and hide from the shallow superficialities of social life. However, Abba Serinus reminds us that the purpose of the cell is to cultivate our way of being when we are outside our cell, as well. The desert elders placed great emphasis on integrity and congruence between the inner and outer life. What we practice in our quiet prayer must have an impact on how we interact with others in the world. "The reality of the cell should spill over into the reality of our life. The boundaries of our cell are gradually expanded to include every moment in our life and every detail in our world" (John Chryssavgis, *In the Heart of the Desert*, 43).

7 Using the terms "father" and "son" was indicative of a close bond between the monks, similar to the relationship between master and disciple.

8 The cell is both an interior place where we encounter God in the deepest recesses of our hearts and an exterior place that holds us in this inner exploration. We often need quiet spaces and times of retreat to really connect with the sacred within.

✳ Much of my own work and personal journey is about exploring what it means to be a monk in the world. Rather than live my life within the walls of a monastery, I choose to live in the heart of the city, doing all the ordinary things that are necessary like grocery shopping, balancing my checkbook, walking my dog, connecting with neighbors, being fully present in my marriage and friendships, even when struggles arise. This story from the desert fathers is the essence of this call. Being a monk in the world means finding the sacred presence everywhere. We begin with our inner cell, and slowly we discover that the holy radiates from every corner. In Benedictine tradition the kitchen utensils are considered as holy as the vessels of the altar. The stranger knocking at the door is thought to represent Christ.

They said of Abba Serinus that he used to work hard and always ate two small loaves. Abba Job, his companion and himself a great ascetic, went to see him and said, "I am careful about what I do in the cell, but when I come out I do as the brothers do." Abba Serinus said to him, "There is no great virtue in keeping to your regime in your cell, but there is if you keep it when you come out of your cell."[6]

(SERINUS 1)

One day Abba Daniel and Abba Ammoes went on a journey together. Abba Ammoes said, "When shall we, too, settle down in a cell, Father?"[7] Abba Daniel replied, "Who shall separate us henceforth from God? God is in the cell,[8] and, on the other hand, he is outside also."

(DANIEL 5)

9   Amma Theodora is referring to this passage in the Christian scriptures: "Enter through the narrow gate; for the gate is wide and the road is easy that leads to destruction, and there are many who take it. For the gate is narrow and the road is hard that leads to life, and there are few who find it" (Matthew 7:13–14). The concept of the monastic cell is a literal reality, a place where the monks retreated to experience a deep stillness; yet, it is also the symbolic place within us where we welcome in the fullness of our experience. Much of the desert journey is about becoming fully present to our emotional life and the feelings and voices with which we do battle. The gate is narrow because there are few who are brave enough to enter this inner cell and stay present within these figurative storms.

10   We might contemplate this inner cell in the wake of the terrible events around the world. It can be overwhelming to listen to the news and feel our smallness in the face of things. And yet, the call is to stand "before the winter's storms." Standing and staying present to our own experience, making space to feel this grief, welcoming in our feelings of helplessness, raging at injustice, we are asked to let it all in. Only by becoming fully present to our own suffering can we respond with full compassion to the suffering of others.

Gregory Mayers writes in *Listen to the Desert*:

> In times of inner turmoil and in the urgency to find a resolution to the confusion or an escape from it, rather than be hostage to your anguish, be attentive to the process as it is happening. Be attentive to the shame and fear, the emptiness and despondency, with which the ego greets the dawning wholeness. Take the middle course during the stormy period of transformation. Don't tamper with it. Let it happen. Let go. (p. 50)

When we face this magnitude of suffering we are moved to the question of "why"? Yet we are also called to recognize that we do not know the answer; we rest in humility rather than theological platitudes. We may want to try and make sense of it in order to obtain a feeling of control, yet that is another way we run away from the fierceness of the storm.

Amma Theodora said, "Let us strive to enter by the narrow gate.[9] Just as the trees, if they have not stood before the winter's storms[10] cannot bear fruit, so it is with us; this present age is a storm and it is only through many trials and temptations that we can obtain an inheritance in the kingdom of heaven."

(THEODORA 2)

11 The cell calls us to stay in the mind as well as in the body. We can be in a place physically, and yet our thoughts might be far away. Unless we can find God here in the cell, there is no point in going anywhere else.

12 This excerpt is drawn from Rowan Williams, *Silence and Honey Cakes*, p. 89.

✳ The desert elders call us to make a commitment to sit in silence with whatever rises up. Sometimes that time is filled with abiding stillness, but more often there are waves of emotion rising, unexpected feelings that we would rather not experience. The emotions are a bridge between our minds and bodies. When we feel sad or angry, we experience these both as thoughts and as experiences in our bodies. What we often do is let our thoughts carry us far away from our actual experience and avoid feeling deeply what is happening in our body. This is the call of the desert: to sit with our own experience, to be true to what is rising up within us and allow it space to move through rather than resisting it, and to become aware of our thoughts and the ways they distract us from life. The desert is not just a place, but a whole way of life, one that calls us to radical presence with ourselves and deep honesty about our inner experience.

✳ I love the horizon-broadening adventure of travel and the invitation of pilgrimage within me to go to unexplored places. The purpose of these voyages, however, is always to return home again, carrying the new insight back to everyday life. The desert fathers and mothers remind us that the journey we take in our monk's cell—which is really a metaphor for the inner cell of our hearts—is the adventure we are called to take day after day, the adventure to be present to God and to the mystery of ourselves that we discover there.

Go. Sit in your cell and give your body[11] in pledge to these walls.

(ANONYMOUS 73)[12]

13 Running away does not help us; we bring along our struggles with us. The desert elders remind us that wherever we go, we ourselves are the same. Our temptation is to believe that a relationship is too challenging, a job is too difficult, a place is too boring, or whatever our inner chatter may tell us. What we discover through the practice of staying where we are, is that these same judgments are always within us, no matter our physical location. These inner demons may take different forms or hues, but the essence will be the same—the gnawing dissatisfaction we feel in life travels with us.

This does not mean that we are never to leave a relationship, or job, or home that is unrewarding (or even worse, is actively destructive). It means that, over time, we become aware of our patterns of responding and relating. We notice what situations "push our buttons" and cause us to have a strong energetic response. These always point to some place within ourselves that is struggling for freedom, that is limited by judgment or wounding. As we grow in awareness, we become intimate with our places of challenge and slowly free ourselves from unconscious reactions rooted in these patterns.

14 This excerpt is drawn from Laura Swan, *The Forgotten Desert Mothers*, p. 35

15 This excerpt is drawn from Rowan Williams, *Silence and Honey Cakes*, p. 85.

We carry ourselves wherever we go and we cannot escape temptation by mere flight.[13]

(MATRONA 1)[14]

Amma Theodora also said, "There was a monk, who, because of the great number of his temptations said, 'I will go away from here.' As he was putting on his sandals, he saw another man who was also putting on his sandals and this other monk said to him, 'Is it on my account you are going away? Because I go before you wherever you are going.'"

(THEODORA 7)

If a trial comes upon you in the place where you live, do not leave that place when the trial comes. Wherever you go, you will find that what you are running from is there ahead of you. So stay until the trial is over, so that if you do end up leaving, no offence will be caused, and you will not bring distress to others who live in the same neighborhood.

(ANONYMOUS 68)[15]

16 Anger was an even more common vice in the desert than sexual temptation. Monks living in the same monastic community likely had vastly different backgrounds—coming from different cultures, social statuses, and education levels—and these differences were often the source of conflict. The sayings reveal that the biggest challenges the monks encountered was with other people and the way different value systems or priorities could cause conflict.

17 Again, this story points to the need to stay put and to work patiently through whatever is causing our anger, approaching it with the humility to know that it is our issue as much as it is someone else "causing" how we feel. When we feel tempted to run away to a proverbial cave, we might ask ourselves if we are fleeing responsibility for our own thoughts and actions.

There was once a brother in a monastery who had a rather turbulent temperament; he often became angry.[16] So he said to himself, "I will go live on my own. If I have nothing to do with anyone else, I shall live in peace and my passions will be soothed." Off he went to live in solitude in a cave. One day when he had filled a jug with water, he put it on the ground and it tipped over. So he picked it up again and filled it again—and again it tipped over. He filled it a third time, put it down and over it went again. He was furious: he grabbed the jug and smashed it. Then he came to his senses and realized that he had been tricked by the devil. He said, "Since I have been defeated, even in solitude, I'd better go back to the monastery. Conflict is to be met everywhere, but so is patience and so is the help of God." So he got up and went back where he came from.[17]

(ANONYMOUS 69)

1 The word for the heart in Greek is *kardia*, and is the place we enter in prayer.

2 The Greek word for salvation is *soteria*, which indicates a sense of wholeness and integrity. To be saved means to find congruence between your inner life and how you are in the world. It means to return to your heart as the source of awareness and attention.

3 For the desert elders, the heart was the source of words and actions. It was considered to be an "axial" organ that centers the physical and spiritual dimensions of human life. The desert elders saw the heart as the center of our being, the place where we encounter God most intimately.

4 This excerpt was drawn from *Pseudo-Macarius, The Fifty Spiritual Homilies and the Great Letter,* an important text in the desert tradition. Pseudo-Macarius was a fourth-century Syrian monk whose true identity is still being debated by scholars, which is why "pseudo" is used before his name.

✳ Even today, the heart is the center of all spiritual life in Eastern monastic spirituality. We read repeatedly metaphors such as this one from Tomáš Špidlík, as quoted in Mary Forman's *Desert Mothers*:

> In Scripture, the heart contains the fullness of the spiritual life, which involves the whole person, with all (one's) faculties and all (one's) activities. (Moreover,) the heart remains a mystery; it is the hidden part of (the hu)man, known only to God. (p. 80)

In her book *The Wisdom Way of Knowing: Reclaiming an Ancient Tradition to Awaken the Heart*, Cynthia Bourgeault writes that the heart in biblical understanding is not "the seat of your personal emotional life. It is not the 'opposite' of the head. Rather it is a sensitive, multispectrum instrument of awareness: a huge realm of mind that includes both mental and affective operations (that is, the ability both to think and to feel) and both conscious and subconscious dimensions."

(continued on page 28)

☐ Heart-Centered Spirituality

Abba Pambo said, "If you have a heart,[1] you can be saved."[2]

(PAMBO 10)

For the heart directs and governs all other organs of the body. And when grace pastures the heart, it rules over all the members and the thoughts.[3] For there, in the heart, the mind abides as well as the thoughts of the soul and all its hopes. This is how grace penetrates throughout all parts of the body.

(PSEUDO-MACARIUS)[4]

Several of these capacities include: "psychic and extrasensory awareness; intuition; wisdom; a sense of unity; aesthetic, qualitative, and creative faculties; and image-forming and symbolic capacities" ([Jossey-Bass, 2003], 85).

In cultivating a heart-centered spirituality, the desert fathers and mothers are nurturing a different way of being in the world from our left-brain, linear, and analytic ways. By shifting our attention to the heart, we open up the possibility for more avenues of experience.

5 Our hearts harden over time as we grow more distant from ourselves and allow the busyness of the world to consume our attention. The invitation again and again is to return to the heart and to recognize the slow work of spiritual practice in softening us, making us more receptive to God's movements. We may not feel it each day, but this image of the stone serves as a reminder of truth. The desert fathers and mothers knew about stones and hard places in the desert. They witnessed the long journey the heart must take through that barren landscape to connect once again to the still voice within.

The desert elders drew on the biblical image of hardness of heart. For example, in Ezekiel 36:26: "A new heart I will give you, and a new spirit I will put within you; and I will remove from your body the heart of stone and give you a heart of flesh."

❋ Books were rare in the ancient desert, and so many of the monks took to memorizing large amounts of scripture, especially the psalms. Learning these texts "by heart" meant that, on a practical level, they needed fewer scrolls and expensive copies of books. On a spiritual level, the passages became a reservoir of wisdom within the heart, always available to draw upon.

Abba Poemen said, "The nature of water is soft, that of stone is hard; but if a bottle is hung above the stone, allowing the water to fall drop by drop, it wears away the stone. So it is with the word of God; it is soft and our heart is hard,[5] but the man who hears the word of God often, opens his heart to God."

(POEMEN 183)

6 This seems so elementary and yet daily we give our hearts over to things that aren't satisfying or renewing. Daily we make choices that draw us away from our deepest passions and desires. Each time we choose to not sit for our time of morning silence, each time we choose to numb ourselves on endless hours of television, each time we choose to withdraw from the ones we love most, each time we eat food that isn't really nourishing to our body or to our senses—these are all ways we give ourselves over to that which doesn't satisfy.

Satisfaction doesn't always mean happiness. For me, to be satisfied means there is a sense of rightness in the experience, a fullness that comes when I recognize how I have been truly present to the moment. When we are satisfied, we feel we have "enough." I feel satisfied when I don't let life just slip by unnoticed.

7 This saying supports us in living closer to the first saying. Say always what is in your heart. Be a person who is transparent. Let your words be in alignment with your truest self. The desert fathers and mothers were deeply concerned with congruence—alignment between our inner convictions and outward actions.

8 Cherubim and seraphim are part of the celestial hierarchy. Cherubim appear in Genesis 3:24 as guardians of God's glory: "He drove out the man; and at the east of the garden of Eden he placed the cherubim, and a sword flaming and turning to guard the way to the tree of life." The Ark of the Covenant was lavishly built with a golden mercy seat flanked by two golden cherubim. Seraphim appear in Isaiah 6:2: "Seraphs were in attendance above him; each had six wings: with two they covered their faces, and with two they covered their feet, and with two they flew." Seraph means "burn," so they were considered to be creatures of fire.

[Abba Poemen] said, "Do not give your heart to that which does not satisfy your heart."[6]

(POEMEN 80)

Abba Poemen said, "Teach your mouth to say what is in your heart."[7]

(POEMEN 164)

Abba Bessarion, at the point of death, said, "The monk ought to be as the Cherubim and the Seraphim: all eye."[8]

(BESSARION 11)

9   In Paul's Letter to the Ephesians he prays that the eyes of the heart might be opened (1:18). Seeing with these eyes is different from our usual way of seeing. It draws upon the integrative function of the heart and calls us to wonder at the world. We often move through life skimming the surface with our eyes. Our eyes become tired and blurry, and we no longer see the sacred shimmering before us. As the poet David Whyte writes in his poem "Sweet Darkness," "when your eyes are tired / the world is tired also" (excerpted from *The House of Belonging* [Many Rivers Press, 1997]). The desert elders call us to renew our vision, to align our seeing with the holy presence everywhere.

10   This excerpt is drawn from John Cassian, *Conferences*, I. xiii.

❋   My eyes become especially tired after staring at a computer screen all day. I love how technology makes editing so simple (I can remember my mother typing her dissertation when I was a very young child, re-typing pages each time she made changes). I love how the World Wide Web connects me with people around the world and offers me multiple ways to share my work. But my eyes can easily glaze over after too many hours. Even the best things need to be held in balance. I renew my vision by walking outside, connecting with the flesh-and-blood reality of the world around me, playing with my dog, feeling my heart beat more loudly as I climb the hills in my neighborhood.

These sayings invite us to remember to always return to the wisdom of the heart, to orient ourselves again and again through our center, so that we might see clearly once again. We constantly fall away from our center through habits and distractions. The desert elders remind us to return again and again to this place of graced vision.

Abba Moses of Skete says: "Whenever the gaze strays even a little, we should turn back the eyes of the heart[9] into the straight line towards [God]."

JOHN CASSIAN[10]

11 Desert father Evagrius Ponticus believed that knowing the types of demons a monk experienced could, with spiritual discernment, lead to a transforming self-knowledge and openness that he called "purity of heart." Other desert elders called this *kardio-gnosis*, or knowledge of one's heart.

Purity of heart is another important theme in the desert literature. It was considered to be "a person's most authentic state-of-being" (David G. R. Keller, *Oasis of Wisdom*, 25). Purification occurs in many ways—for example, through the cleansing power of tears of compunction, or by releasing the hold of our thoughts and ideas. We continue to release the hold of ideas until we have become a vessel open entirely to God's grace. Non-attachment is also essential. I explore each of these themes later in the book.

12 This text refers back to the idea of congruence and knowing the heart's true motivations. We do not cultivate a holy life for the approval of others. Often, it is our desire to make everyone else happy that causes us to be torn apart. When we seek an inward kind of satisfaction, one in which we are true to God's calling in our hearts, only then can we find peace.

Amma Sarah said, "If I prayed God that all men should approve of my conduct I should find myself a penitent at the door of each one, but I shall rather pray that my heart may be pure[11] towards all."[12]

(SARAH 5)

1 Passions in Greek is *pathe*, which is derived from *pathos*, meaning "suffering" or "disease." However, passions are much more than sins or vices. They are our inner wounds, what theologian John Chryssavgis calls "those deep marks in the spaces of our heart that require healing" (*In the Heart of the Desert*, 53). Passions call us to embrace our vulnerability and brokenness. This is the desert path toward healing and wholeness—being honest about that with which we struggle.

Passions are the "shifting, unfree, unintegrated part of ourselves" (Alan Jones, *Soul Making,* 104). These "impure thoughts" are also referred to by the term *logismoi*. They include the eight thoughts that desert father Evagrius says every monk must battle: gluttony, lust, anger, avarice, sadness, *acedia*, vain-glory, and pride. Upon going into the desert to free oneself of the responsibilities of daily life and seek the peace of *hesychia*, one was also stepping into a space where one could come face to face with these thoughts. In solitude, monks had to face the daily assaults of discouragement and lethargy in spiritual practice and life, as well as the force of anger or lust. Of course, we encounter these same passions in our lives. Our experience of these inner forces often feels like a wilderness place. This is where the metaphor of desert as an interior reality becomes especially important.

2 This excerpt is drawn from Zosimas, *Reflections* V ii c. Abba Zosimas was a fifth- to sixth-century desert father living in the Palestinian desert. He is known for discovering and sharing the story of Mary of Egypt.

☐ Thoughts, Desires, and Passions

It was well said once by a wise person, that the soul has as many masters as it has passions.[1] And again, the Apostle says: "People are slaves to whatever masters them" (2 Pet. 2.19).

(ZOSIMAS)[2]

3   The desert elders are our fellow travelers on this narrow and challenging path. This is the root of *ascesis*, or the hard work of being a monk. Their stories speak of moments of peace and then long journeys through struggle with "demons," which indicated a way of understanding the inner and outer forces, temptations, voices, and judgments that lead us away from the heart of God. Demons are those energies that scatter our attention, that disrupt our ability to stay present and centered. The desert fathers and mothers realized early on that their thoughts impacted their actions, and so ascetical practices were a way of facing, rooting out, and letting go of these behaviors and patterns that undermine us. The struggle comes from being really honest with ourselves about what we face within. The knowledge of how to engage in this struggle came slowly, over many years. John Chryssavgis writes in *In the Heart of the Desert*:

> If God is right there, in the midst of our struggle, then our aim is to stay there. We are to remain in the cell, to stay on the road, not to forego the journey or forget the darkness. It is all too easy for us to overlook the importance of struggle, preferring instead to secure peace and rest, or presuming to reach the stage of love prematurely. It is always easier to allow things to pass by, to go on without examination and effort. Yet, struggling means living. It is a way of fully living life and not merely observing it. It takes much time and a great effort to unite the disparate, disjointed, and divided parts of the self into an integrated whole. During this time and in this effort, the virtue of struggle was one of the nonnegotiables in the spiritual way of the desert. The Desert Fathers and Mothers speak to us with authority, because they are in fact our fellow travelers. They never claim to have arrived, they never indicate having completed the journey. (p.104)

The desert elders teach us how to be in relationship with the multitude of chaotic impulses that distract our attention from the still point within us where God is present. This is why so few of us have the

(*continued on page 40*)

Abba Ammonas was asked, "What is the 'narrow and hard way?'" (Matt. 7:14). He replied, "'The narrow and hard way' is this, to control your thoughts, to strip yourself of your own will for the sake of God.[3] This is also the meaning of the sentence, 'Lo, we have left everything and followed you.'" (Matt. 19:27)

(AMMONAS 11)

courage to enter the spirituality of the desert: journeying toward God means showing up fully for our inner struggles, engaging with them fully, coming to terms with our wounds and inner divisions, and doing the hard, slow work of healing.

4 This story is referring to 1 Samuel 17:34–36.

5 One of the primary attitudes toward the passions in the desert was to consider them something to be eradicated. The lifelong struggle is to eliminate passions from our experience. From this perspective they are considered disordered and with the devil as their source.

6 The desert elders regularly use the metaphor of "battle" for the spiritual life. Amma Syncletica counsels courage and hard work in this "battle." I resist that kind of violent imagery. And yet, in Benedictine monk and scholar Michael Casey's *A Guide to Living in the Truth: Saint Benedict's Teaching on Humility*, he writes that "a much more creative way of dealing with difficult texts is to take our negative reaction as an indication that there may be an issue beneath the surface with which we must deal" ([Liguri Publications/Triumph Books, 2001], 5).

When we experience resistance to what we are reading, we need to pay attention to what is being stirred within us.

[Abba Poemen] said, "David, when he was fighting with the lion,[4] seized it by the throat and killed it immediately. If we take ourselves by the throat and by the belly, with the help of God, we shall overcome the invisible lion."

(POEMEN 178)

Abba Joseph asked Abba Sisoes, "For how long must a man cut away the passions?" The old man said to him, "Do you want to know how long?" Abba Joseph answered, "Yes." The old man said to him, "So long as a passion attacks you, cut it away at once."[5]

(SISOES 22)

Amma Syncletica said, "In the beginning there are a great many battles[6] and a good deal of suffering for those who are advancing towards God and afterwards, ineffable joy. It is like those who wish to light a fire; at first they are choked by smoke and cry, and by this means obtain what they seek (and it is said: 'Our God is a consuming fire' Heb. 12:29): so we also must kindle the divine fire in ourselves through tears and hard work."

(SYNCLETICA 1)

7 Demons play a large role in desert theology. In Evagrius's *Praktikos*, more than two-thirds of his writing discusses the nature of demons. The eight thoughts (see chapter 4, note 1) are considered to be demons at work. This does not mean he thought of demons as purely psychological realities. According to theologian William Harmless, Evagrius and the other desert ascetics believed in the reality of demons whose most common method of warfare with the desert dwellers was through their thoughts (see William Harmless, *Desert Christians: An Introduction to the Literature of Early Monasticism* [New York: Oxford University Press, 2004], 327). He recommended that monks engage in watchfulness (or *nepsis*, as we explored earlier) in order to observe the intensity of their thoughts, watching them rise and fall. Wisdom is won only through battle—often with a demon.

✳ We might also remember that "battle" is an archetypal idea, with the warrior as an ancient expression of the one who goes to battle. Warrior energy is something we all carry within us to varying degrees; it calls us to be fierce protectors of our boundaries. The warrior in each of us is able to say yes and no very clearly. The desert elders lived in a fierce landscape that reminded them again and again to strip away the inessentials. This is always a painful process and hard work. This text reinforces the need to stay with our thoughts in fierce and patient battle. Staying with ourselves and our experience is the only way through.

Often we set out on the contemplative path with great hopes for inner peace. But we soon discover that quieting ourselves down to really listen to the voices within can be overwhelming or unnerving. We may begin to think that we are better off humming along life's surface, or that we have "monkey-mind" and sitting in silence just seems to make things worse. We feel frustrated, even dismayed perhaps. We start to lose focus in our practice.

Certainly those who practice contemplative ways of living may experience, over time, a greater sense of equanimity. However, the pathway to the heart of deep peace is through challenging terrain—our own inner worlds. In the silence, we are invited to become intimate with all

(continued on page 44)

Abba Joseph put the same question and Abba Poemen said to him, "If someone shuts a snake and a scorpion in a bottle, in time they will be completely destroyed. So it is with evil thoughts: they are suggested by the demons;[7] they disappear through patience."

(POEMEN 21)

our shortcomings, all our judgments about self and others, all the desires we have for things or comforts that seem to lead away from God.

8 This excerpt is drawn from John Chryssavgis's *Reflections*, IV a.

9 Another perspective from the elders on the passions was to view them as something positive, as natural impulses, rather than originating from the devil. In fact, many of the desert elders believed that the source of the passions was from God, and when passions were directed toward their purpose, only then were they free from tyranny. In this view, "the aim is to illumine them, not eliminate them; they are not to be destroyed but mastered and even transfigured" (John Chryssavgis, *In the Heart of the Desert*, 56). Our passions are simply our energies, misdirected. When our passions are distorted, then we feel divided. When we are able to realign ourselves with God, we become integrated and whole again. Our true passion is an energy that can direct us back to the sacred source of our being.

John Chryssavgis refers to a powerful passage from Abba Isaiah in his *Ascetic Discourses*, where he claims that all of the passions, including anger and jealousy, are actually bestowed by God with a sacred purpose and direction. Because we have misdirected the passions, they have become distorted. Anger was originally for the purpose of fighting injustice, jealousy for the purpose of imitating the behavior of the saints. (ibid., 57)

10 This excerpt is drawn from Zosimas, *Reflections* X d.

✳ In more contemporary language, we might consider the passions as distorted when the ego is in control of their direction. Then, we desire whatever fills the ego, whether praise, or power, or whatever it is that we crave. When we feel enslaved by what we desire, then we know we have gone down the wrong path. The spiritual journey is always one toward freedom, and an essential aspect is to direct the passions and desire toward God. The more we become clear about our places of wounding, the more freedom we gain because we are no longer controlled by unconscious impulses.

Some brothers happened one day to meet at Abba Joseph's cell. While they were sitting there, questioning him, he became cheerful and, filled with happiness he said to them, "I am king today, for I reign over the passions."

(JOSEPH OF PANEPHYSIS 10)

[Abba Zosimas] used to say: "Take away the thoughts, and no one can become holy. One who avoids the beneficial temptation is avoiding eternal life."[8]

It is like I always say: Inasmuch as He is good, God has given us to profit from everything.[9] However we become attached and misuse God's gifts; and so we turn these very same good gifts to destruction through our evil choice, and are therefore harmed.[10]

(*continued on page 47*)

11 The desert elders call us to a radical reclaiming of full responsibility for ourselves. I am comforted by their words: we all will experience temptation and we should expect to experience it until we die. Contemplative practice does not mean we live perfect lives, free of judgmental thoughts. It means that we are called day-by-day, moment by moment, to be fully conscious and present to our inner world. The monastic way asks that we gently and compassionately witness what happens in our minds and hearts with each encounter. The person at work who really annoys us can challenge us to become curious about the thoughts they evoke and we can slowly work to release those thoughts, rather than allow ourselves to get trapped in a spiral of judgment.

With each breath we can grow more intimate with our own inner landscape. The more we take responsibility for this and keep ourselves from distraction, the more peace we will find. We may even begin to develop a sense of humor about ourselves. When I notice myself in familiar patterns and habits of judgment, I try to bring a spaciousness to the experience, so that I can be present to what is happening.

I say with some lightheartedness, "Oh, there I go again, I am so curious about why I do that." In one of the yoga classes I attend, the yoga teacher often invites us to notice those voices of judgment and say, "Hello, Frustration (or name your judgment of choice), how are you today?" In this way we create room for observing our patterns without getting hooked by them. We are then much freer to not act on our thoughts, but instead allow them to become a window into deeper wisdom about ourselves.

Abba Anthony said to Abba Poemen, "This is the great work of a man: always to take the blame for his own sins before God and to expect temptation to the last breath."[11]

He also said, "Whoever has not experienced temptation cannot enter the Kingdom of Heaven." He even added, "Without temptation no-one can be saved."

(ANTHONY 4–5)

12 These two stories from Ammas Theodora and Syncletica ask us to consider integrity. We have heard the saying "practice what you preach" and probably experienced how hard that can be. When we are in the position of teacher—and that comes in many forms, sometimes as a parent, sometimes as a pastor, sometimes as a leader of another kind—it is imperative that we engage in deep inner work and self-reflection so that our lives might be witness to our teachings.

✳ One of the greatest gifts I have found in being a spiritual director, teacher, writer, and supervisor of soul care practitioners is that this path calls me to be very honest with myself. If I am to teach about the value of contemplative ways of being and advocate for radical self-care, I had better begin with myself. I am called each day to renew my commitment to these practices. Often the shadow side of teaching is neglecting to make the time or space for the very principles you espouse to others.

Living a life of integrity demands this kind of inner commitment. The desert elders were conscious of their role as teachers in the community, even if they never stepped foot in the classroom. They lived their lives as witnesses to different ways of being in the world, ways of being that cultivated presence and peace both within and without.

The virtues of true spiritual elders are patience, gentleness, and humility. These virtues demonstrate freedom from a particular agenda and a deep openness to the work of the spirit in souls.

[Amma Theodora] said that a teacher ought to be a stranger to the desire for domination, vain-glory, and pride; one should not be able to fool him by flattery, nor blind him by gifts. Nor conquer by the stomach, nor dominate him by anger; but he should be patient, gentle and humble as far as possible; he must be rested and without partisanship, full of concern, and a lover of souls.

(THEODORA 5)

[Amma Syncletica] said, "It is dangerous for anyone to teach who has not first been trained in the 'practical' life. For if someone who owns a ruined house receives guests there, he does them harm because of the dilapidation of his dwelling. It is the same in the case of someone who has not first built an interior dwelling; he causes loss to those who come. By words one may convert them to salvation, but by evil behavior, one injures them."

(SYNCLETICA 12)[12]

13 Each of us encounters the power of destruction in our lives: the time when a loved one dies, or we receive a diagnosis of serious illness, or we lose a dream, a job, or an identity. Our temptation is to pretend it doesn't hurt as much as it does. We want to run toward our favorite way to numb the pain.

The paradox in the spiritual life is that this journey through destruction is necessary to reach any kind of resurrection or new life beyond it. We are rebuilt and reshaped through this process. We must fully surrender ourselves to the awfulness of it. We must stay present with how we feel and bring compassion to ourselves in the process. We must learn to no longer feel victim to our suffering, but to instead discover a kind of inner fierceness that allows us to look death in the eye without flinching.

The desert fathers and mothers tell us to do this through practice, day-by-day, staying with the smaller kinds of grief that arise all the time. We stay with our breath, using it as an anchor in this moment. We allow the fullness of the feelings to move through our bodies. The only way through grief is to take the journey right into its heart. Anything less and we continue to suffer much longer than we need to.

Abba Alonius said, "If I had not destroyed myself completely, I should not have been able to rebuild and shape myself again."[13]

(ALONIUS 2)

[Abba Nilus] said, "Whatever you have endured out of love of wisdom will bear fruit for you at the time of prayer."

(NILUS 2, 5)

14 | *Accidie* (also spelled *acedia*) is often translated as sloth. Evagrius described it as a kind of restlessness, boredom, and sense of discouragement in the spiritual life. In the *Praktikos*, as quoted in William Harmless's *Desert Christians*, Evagrius describes it this way:

> The demon of *acedia*—also called the noonday demon—is the one that causes the most trouble of all. He presses his attack upon the monk about the fourth hour and besieges the soul until the eighth hour. First he makes it seem that the sun barely moves, if at all, and that the day is fifty hours long. (pp. 324–25)

He goes on to write that this demon causes the monk to pace and look outside impatiently, trying to figure out when the workday is done. It causes the monk to confront the sameness of his life. The monk struggling with this demon longs for a distraction or escape.

Accidie is the doubt that creeps in about our call in life, or about the meaning of it all. It is a form of deep anxiety that paralyzes us. Often we think, "I could be more holy if only my life weren't filled with distractions." This tempting thought of waiting until life has all the right circumstances is an example of *acedia*. The practice of the desert fathers and mothers is to remember that each moment is holy and to bring our full attention to everything we do as sacred.

The only cure for *acedia* is to stay with one's practice; to return again and again to prayer. Evagrius counsels the monk afflicted by this listlessness to actively wrestle with it. The way of the desert is an interior journey, and at the heart of it is a willingness to explore the dungeons and dark corners of the psyche without looking away.

When the holy Abba Anthony lived in the desert he was beset by accidie,[14] and attacked by many sinful thoughts. He said to God, "Lord, I want to be saved but these thoughts do not leave me alone; what shall I do in my affliction? How can I be saved?" A short while afterwards, when he got up to go out, Anthony saw a man like himself sitting at his work, getting up from his work to prayer. It was an angel of the Lord sent to correct and reassure him. He heard the angel saying to him, "Do this and you will be saved." At these words, Anthony was filled with joy and courage. He did this, and he was saved.

(ANTHONY 1)

A brother asked Abba Poemen about accidie. The old man said to him, "Accidie is there every time one begins something, and there is no worse passion, but if a man recognizes it for what it is, he will gain peace."

(POEMEN 149)

15 We all have our inner versions of these "evil thoughts." They tend to run us in circles, keeping us from the deep peace we long for. They can affect our physical health as well. Consider the times you have made a commitment to a spiritual practice and then came down with a cold, and quickly you forgot the fervor of your commitment. They are the thoughts that cause us to get up before our prayer time is done because nothing seems to be happening. The process of becoming fully at peace is a long, slow process of bringing back all the pieces of our fragmented selves. If we recognize what is happening to us, as Abba Poemen suggests, then we can free ourselves from the hook of evil thoughts.

Kathleen Norris writes in *Acedia and Me: A Marriage, Monks, and a Writer's Life*:

> ... much of the restless boredom, frantic escapism, commitment phobia, and enervating despair that plagues us today is *acedia* in modern dress. The boundaries between depression and *acedia* are notoriously fluid; at the risk of oversimplifying, I would suggest that depression is an illness treatable by counseling and medication, *acedia* is a vice that is best countered by spiritual practice and the discipline of prayer. (p. 3)

Norris's book is an intriguing exploration of the personal and cultural implications of this ancient idea. She suggests that much of what creates anxiety and dissatisfaction in our modern lives has to do with *acedia*. Her distinction with depression is a subtle yet helpful one. According to Norris, *acedia* is not the same as depression and can only be treated through doing exactly the opposite of what it tempts us to do. When *acedia* is at work we think our spiritual practice is useless or boring; we have no motivation. And yet discipline and showing up for practice is precisely what we need to do to combat its effects on our thoughts and motivations.

[Amma Theodora] said, "It is good to live in peace, for the wise man practices perpetual prayer.... However you should realize that as soon as you intend to live in peace, at once evil comes down and weighs on your soul through accidie, faintheartedness, and evil thoughts.[15] It also attacks your body through sickness, debility, weakening of the knees, and all the members. It dissipates the strength of soul and body, so that one believes one is ill and no longer able to pray. But if we are vigilant, all these temptations fall away."

(THEODORA 3)

1 Excerpt drawn from David G. R. Keller, *Oasis of Wisdom*, p. 139.

※ The desert monks tried to practice what the Buddhists call "beginner's mind." In Benedict's Rule, which is described as a "little rule for beginners," Benedict writes, "always we begin again." Remembering this, we are less likely to get caught up in our own hubris about the spiritual life. The desert monks invite us again and again to commit to our spiritual practice and path.

This is the essence of humility—to remember that we are always beginning in the spiritual life (Rule of Benedict, 73:8). The moment we think that we have it all "figured out," the further we are from the spiritual path. Humility demands that we always come to our journey with a spirit of openness, knowing that there is always more to learn. Conversely, when we think we have fallen away too far to return, we may be doomed to never try at all. The path of humility is about holding these two dimensions in balance: being open to always discovering more and always beginning again when we stumble and fall. When we reject both of these, we have lost our way completely.

Committing to a spiritual practice is in part about letting go of the ego's power over us. Without even realizing it, we often begin a regular prayer practice with self-centered motives that are often unconscious, such as wanting to be special, or to feel good about ourselves, or even as an antidote to living in the modern world. Over time, however, these motives will be revealed through practice and our ego will experience disillusionment and want to walk away. In *Listen to the Desert*, Gregory Mayers writes that it is the very times that we want to quit our spiritual practice, when we're plagued with boredom or dissatisfaction and manage to work through them, that we find the essence of what the desert fathers and mothers were talking about. We recommit ourselves; we begin again. As Thomas Merton wrote in *The Wisdom of the Desert*, "There are only three stages to this work: to be a beginner, to be more of a beginner, and to be only a beginner" (p. 30).

☐ Humility, Simplicity, and the Beginner's Heart

Abba Poemen said about Abba Pior that every single day he made a fresh beginning.

(POEMEN)[1]

Abba Moses asked Abba Silvanus, "Can a man lay a new foundation every day?" The old man said, "If he works hard he can lay a new foundation at every moment."

(SILVANUS 11)

2 Theophilus was patriarch of Alexandria, Egypt, from 385 to 412 CE during a time of conflict between the newly dominant Christians and the existing pagan establishment. He had a close relationship with the desert fathers in Egypt and especially those in the community at Scete.

3 The monastery in the Scetis valley of Egypt became a center where many monks gathered and where the famous monk John Cassian lived for many years. Skete became the name for a particular kind of monastic dwelling that allowed for the relative solitude of individual monks but provided them with space to come together for prayer, sharing resources, and safety.

4 Excerpt drawn from Thomas Merton, *The Wisdom of the Desert*, 168 CXXX.

✳ Father Gregory Mayers approaches desert wisdom through the contemporary language of ego. He describes the deep trance we all succumb to which is the idolization of ourselves and our ego. What we desire in life becomes the motivating force for our actions. When we make choices from the ego, what we know about ourselves is reinforced. Anything that doesn't fit with our self-identification is rejected. The desert fathers and mothers invite us to strip away our thoughts and these outward identities. Mayers writes in *Listen to the Desert*:

> Thinking and the deep self-trance are as inseparable as up and down, left and right, and cold and heat.... The question of vital importance is: "What can I do to dispel the trance?" He goes on to say that we must take up the practice of "nonthinking," which is a matter of "overcoming the *habitual conflict* that composes thinking." (pp. 22–23)

In this story, Abba Pambo recognizes that he could try and offer up many words of wisdom to the bishop, however it might serve only his ego to appear wise. Actions may be powerful, but sometimes letting go of our need to appear a certain way is more authentic than if we acted from our ego needs.

Theophilus of holy memory, Bishop of Alexandria,[2] journeyed to Scete,[3] and the brethren coming together said to Abba Pambo: "Say a word or two to the Bishop, that his soul may be edified in this place." The elder replied: "If he is not edified by my silence, there is no hope he will be edified by my words."[4]

A brother in Scetis committed a fault. A council was called to which Abba Moses was invited, but he refused to go to it. Then the priest sent someone to say to him, "Come, for everyone is waiting for you." So he got up and went. He took a leaking jug, filled it with water and carried it with him. The others came out to meet him and said to him, "What is this, Father?" The old man said to them, "My sins run out behind me, and I do not see them, and today I am coming to judge the errors of another." When they heard that they said no more to the brother but forgave him.

(MOSES 2)

✳ Jesus advised those who are without sin to cast the first stone (John 8:7). To hold back judgment of others requires great humility. It requires us to recognize our own sinfulness and woundedness before we rush to judge another. So often, in psychological terms, what we hate in another person is what we hate in ourselves. This is called projection, where our own shadow material is so repugnant to us that we frequently identify it in the exterior world. Humility is the act of remembering our earthiness and limitations.

Preoccupation with the sins of others blinds us to our own failings. When we claim the wholeness of our experience we become more compassionate toward others. Abba Moses is practicing humility here, and approaches his brother from a profound sense of his own brokenness.

5 We often bring unconscious expectations to life. We feel disappointed when things don't turn out as we had hoped, even when we aren't aware we had a desire for a particular outcome. Often we are poor judges of what "should" happen in our lives. We bring a whole set of ego-centered habits and patterns, and we dream from the person that we have been, rather than the person we are being transformed into. Our transformed self is always far beyond our own strivings.

When we recognize that we have limited vision and that our planning minds will only take us so far (and I am someone who loves to plan!), then we can begin to gently release the pressure we put on ourselves to have things turn out a certain way. We may begin to approach life in a more open-hearted way, receiving its gifts rather than grumbling about what we would rather have had happen. There is a much bigger wisdom at work in the wide expanse of night dreams than we can perceive in the light of day.

In yoga philosophy there are two concepts related to this: *satya*, which means truth, and *santosha*, which means contentment. These two concepts ask us: Can we accept the truth of what is in this moment without wanting it to be different? This doesn't mean that when genuine injustice is being perpetrated we don't respond. It means that first we accept the truth of the experience; we let ourselves really feel it.

(continued on page 62)

[Abba Nilus] said, "Do not be always wanting everything to turn out as you think it should,[5] but rather as God pleases, then you will be undisturbed and thankful in your prayer."

(NILUS 7)

Then, once we embrace what is, we are able to find some contentment there. This doesn't mean being happy at any cost, but points to an ability to find ease and gentleness in the moment. Can we be content that we have a source much greater than ourselves to offer us wisdom about life? The desert fathers and mothers invite us to let go of what we expect to have happen and cultivate a sense of gratitude and contentment with whatever actually is happening.

6 Fasting is one aspect of the asceticism to which the desert monks devoted themselves. Asceticism essentially is about letting go of everything that keeps us from God; it is considered a journey toward authentic freedom. Desert ascetics kept their possessions to a minimum, and fasting was practiced as a way of attending to the needs of the body. Fasting to the point of harm to the body was condemned, although there were certainly monks who did end up starving themselves to death.

The desert monks lived extraordinarily simply in stone huts, sleeping on reed mats, a sheep-skin for warmth, a lamp to see by, and a container for oil or water (see *Sayings of the Desert Fathers*, xxiii). Food and sleep were reduced to the very minimum needed to sustain them so they could watch for God. They kept silence so they could hear God more clearly. They were committed to supporting themselves completely with the work of their own hands.

Fasting isn't just for its own sake. When we fast from food, we are called to become keenly aware of our relationship to food and to pay attention to our own hungers. When we fast from the comforts of our lives, the invitation is to stretch ourselves and become present to what happens when we don't have our usual securities to rely upon. One meal a day was considered sufficient.

7 Truly savor the food you eat, linger over it, and celebrate the gift of nourishment. Taste and pay attention to whether that is enough.

Abba Daniel used to say, "He lived with us many a long year and every year we used to take him only one basket of bread and when we went to find him the next year we would eat some of that bread."[6]

(ARSENIUS 17)

Abba Daniel used to tell how when Abba Arsenius learned that all the varieties of fruit were ripe he would say, "Bring me some." He would taste very little of each, just once, giving thanks to God.[7]

(ARSENIUS 19)

8   Fasting is an invitation to authentic freedom—freedom from the things that weigh us down or restrict us. These might be material things, such as possessions, or stories and beliefs.

Abba Isidore is speaking here about abstaining from false speech or ideas that keep us from truly living, fasting from that which doesn't truly nourish us in spirit. We all hold onto ideas about ourselves that keep us limited in what we believe we can do with our lives. We all fill our lives with words as a way to avoid what is really happening within us—whether our own words repeating our old stories, or turning up the radio or television and being saturated with the words of others.

✳   I absolutely adore books. They are essential to my work and writing and I can easily justify the many bookcases in our home overflowing with volumes of great wisdom. The problem becomes when I hear about a new book, and I reach to purchase it (so easy to do now in these online times). I have learned to check in with myself: Do I really need this? Am I avoiding embracing my own wisdom by relying on the words of others? This is a delicate balance, because I deeply believe that books open up new worlds, and I am firmly committed to my own ongoing growth.

But, like anything, books can also have a shadow side; we can be tempted into believing we need more information about something in order to feel complete. Sometimes we buy more books as a surrogate for truly living what we believe those books to contain. The key is being fully present to ourselves and noticing where the hunger comes from and distinguishing the direction of our desires.

The invitation from the desert elders here is, first and foremost, to fully live. That will mean something different to each of us, but we have all had the experience of truly coming alive. And we all have ways of avoiding that very thing.

Abba Isidore of Pelusia said, "To live without speaking is better than to speak without living. For the former who lives rightly does good even by his silence but the latter does no good even when he speaks. When words and life correspond to one another they are together the whole of philosophy."[8]

(ISIDORE OF PELUSIA 1)

9 This is a difficult story to read. Yet, the desert fathers and mothers offer us parables and imagery to shape our imaginations so that we are confronted fiercely with their message. This story isn't so much about whether we give up all of our belongings to the poor, for certainly most of us would find that very hard to do, but it is about the call to be single-hearted in our commitment. The root of the word monk is *monos*, which means one or single. It isn't so much about marital status as it is about the condition of one's heart. To live as a monk, we must commit to living our lives with as much integrity as possible. Integrity has the same root as the words integral and integrated: *integritas*, which means wholeness and soundness. To act with integrity means to always be moving toward wholeness and not feeling divided; this is the same meaning as the root of the word monk. The desert calls us to a singleness of heart and to live from this commitment.

10 This saying is included in Alan Jones, *Soul Making*, p. 16.

✳ St. Macarius is demonstrating one of the great virtues of the spiritual life for the desert monks: humility. Derived from the word *humus*, which means "of the earth" or earthiness, to have humility and to be humble is to remember that we are not God. Humility shifts the focus from ourselves to God and to service to others as the center of all things. When we have truly embraced humility, we find ourselves no longer wanting and striving after things, because we discover gratitude and contentment with things exactly as they are. St. Benedict describes humility in great detail in his Rule, ascribing twelve rungs to the ladder of humility, reminding us that humility is a process of growth and always a journey.

In *Soul Wilderness*, Kerry Walters discusses the great irony of the spiritual life:

> When we feel more secure, powerful, confident, and self-sufficient, we are nothing. We are most abjectly *not*. But when we're stripped naked by desert despair, helplessly and hopelessly decreated by all

(*continued on page 68*)

A brother renounced the world and gave his goods to the poor, but he kept back a little for his personal expenses. He went to see Abba Anthony. When he told him this, the old man said to him, "If you want to be a monk, go to the village, buy some meat, cover your naked body with it and come here like that." The brother did so, and the dogs and birds tore at his flesh. When he came back the old man asked him whether he had followed his advice. He showed him his wounded body, and Saint Anthony said, "Those who renounce the world but want to keep something for themselves are torn this way by the demons who make war on them."[9]

(ANTHONY 20)

One day one of the young men asked him: "Abba, tell us about being a monk." And the wisest of monks replied: "Ah! I'm not a monk myself, but I have seen them."

(ST. MACARIUS)[10]

of our facades and deceptions, we are most real, most substantial.
We *are*. Our being is in proportion to the destitution forced on us
by the wilderness. (p. 80)

This is the grace of humility: remembering that we are so much more
than what we cling to, that the way we identify ourselves has little to
do with the truth of who we are.

There is a kind of spiritual death that happens in the desert, this
"decreation" that Walters describes, a kind of contraction of our false
selves, so that our true self can expand into God.

11 Practices like fasting, prayer, and solitude are not magic pills to end
our inner struggles. If anything, they help to heighten our awareness
of our demons by removing the distractions and ways of numbing
ourselves so that our attention can be focused on those demons.

[Amma Theodora] also said that neither asceticism, nor vigils nor any kind of suffering are able to save, only true humility can do that.[11] There was an anchorite who was able to banish the demons; and he asked them, "What makes you go away? Is it fasting?" They replied, "We do not eat or drink." "Is it vigils?" They replied, "We do not sleep." "Is it separation from the world?" "We live in the deserts." "What power sends you away then?" They said, "Nothing can overcome us, but only humility." "Do you see how humility is victorious over demons?"

(THEODORA 6)

12 While the desert fathers and mothers practiced fasting as a regular spiritual discipline, Lent was a season for even greater commitment and austerity. Paul the Simple is working on a single basket, making and remaking it, not as a way of simply creating more work for himself, but as a way of staying present to each moment. Working on the basket becomes an anchor for meditation.

✳ This story of Abba Paul reminds us again of the radical call to simplicity in the desert.

One year, as I gathered my belongings together and packed my bags for a retreat in the desert of New Mexico, I prayed. Was each item necessary? What function did it serve? What would happen if I left it behind? I tried to bring as little as I could (which still included an embarrassing array of comforts).

Often when I travel I pack lightly. When my husband and I have journeyed across Europe to visit ancestral homelands, we drag our bags from place to place, packing and repacking as we go. If we find something we want to bring home, we ask if there is something else we can leave behind in order to make room for it. I like to think of this as a metaphor for our lives.

For the desert fathers and mothers, it wasn't meant to be a competition in asceticism (although certainly that would happen at times). The commitment to simplicity was a way of always focusing on what was essential and letting go of the rest. In this process we let go of what gets in the way of our relationship to God.

It was said of Abba Paul that he spent the whole of Lent eating only one measure of lentils, drinking one small jug of water, and working on one single basket, weaving it and unweaving it, living alone until the feast.[12]

(PAUL THE SIMPLE 4)

13 This refers to his walking stick.

14 I find this to be another one of the desert sayings that is hard to read and embrace. Thieves come and steal Abba Euprepius's belongings (I imagine he didn't have a lot to begin with), and when he discovers they didn't take everything, he runs after them to make sure they do.

15 From the perspective of the desert, those who love the world and the ways of the world are more prone to falling from the spiritual life. An essential aspect of the desert way is to release ourselves from attachments to things and ideas and discover greater freedom in the process.

16 This calls to mind a poem by seventeenth-century Japanese poet and samurai Mizuta Masahide:

> *Since my house burned down*
>
> *I now own a better view*
>
> *of the rising moon*

Anytime we have a desert experience in our lives, something is stripped away. The experience may bring a loss of possessions, loss of identity, or loss of a loved one. We are meant to feel grief over these, to fully experience the pain that comes in these moments. This stripping away forces us to return to the essence of all things. We are thrust into the arms of what is most sacred to us.

Practicing this kind of letting go each day, whether it be disengaging from our own possessions and consuming less or giving more to those in need, letting go of the hold that our compulsive thoughts have on us or releasing expectations, all of these prepare us for the bigger moments of letting go. We might even experience the grace of being grateful for our new view of the moon.

The same old man helped some thieves when they were stealing. When they had taken away what was inside his cell, Abba Euprepius saw that they had left his stick[13] and he was sorry. So he took it and ran after them to give it to them. But the thieves did not want to take it, fearing that something would happen to them if they did. So he asked someone he met who was going the same way to give the stick to them.[14]

Abba Euprepius said "Bodily things are compounded of matter. He who loved the world loved occasions of falling.[15] Therefore if we happen to lose something, we must accept this with joy and gratitude, realizing that we have been set free from care."[16]

(EUPREPIUS 2–3)

17 "I die daily" is from 1 Corinthians 15:31.

18 This saying is drawn from *Life of Anthony* by Athanasius. Athanasius, a bishop of Alexandria, wrote St. Anthony's biography; most of what we know about Anthony's life comes from this source. Athanasius's sayings about St. Anthony helped to spread the concept of monasticism.

❋ Every year on Ash Wednesday, Christians gather together to hear a version of these words: "You are dust, and to dust you shall return" (Genesis 3:19). They are uttered over and over as ash, a potent symbol of death, is smudged on each person's forehead. This practice is a stark reminder of our mortality, because paradoxically when we remember ourselves to be mortal and vulnerable beings, our lives become more radiant with each gifted moment.

The desert monks knew this in a special way; they lived in a harsh and barren landscape, where death was visible all around them. The desert elders don't ask us to face our mortality day after day as a morbid act of fatalism, but as a way of claiming the preciousness of our days.

I once had a pulmonary embolism, which felt very much like a near-death experience. That very real encounter with the possibility that I could die still vibrates within me. Knowing not just the possibility of death but the absolute certain reality that one day I will die has shaken my foundations in all the ways that a desert experience does. Remembering that "I die daily" is another commitment to radical simplicity and humility in the spiritual life.

Abba Anthony said, "Therefore my children, let us hold to the discipline, and not be careless. For we have the Lord for our co-worker in this, as it is written, God works for good with everyone who chooses the good. And in order that we not become negligent, it is good to carefully consider the Apostle's statement: I die daily."[17, 18]

19 *The Ladder of Divine Ascent*, written by John Climacus (570–649 CE), is an important text for early monasticism. The metaphors of the ladder and of keeping death ever before one's eyes figure strongly in desert and monastic spirituality. We are exhorted to remain firmly focused on our unity with God. Being mindful of eventual death need not be morbid, but calls us to always return to that which is essential. To ascend the ladder was to draw closer in intimacy with the Divine.

20 Death of any kind is rarely a welcome experience. Even when we witness the mysteries of nature reveal the glories of springtime that emerge from winter's fallow landscape, we resist death; we try to numb ourselves from life's inevitable stripping away of our "secure" frameworks. We spend so much energy and money attempting to stay young. But when we turn to face death wide-eyed and fully present, when we feel the fullness of the grief it brings, we also slowly begin to discover the new life awaiting us.

[Amma Sarah] also said, "I put my foot out to ascend the ladder,[19] and I place death[20] before my eyes before going up it."

(SARAH 6)

21 Spiritual writer Alan Jones describes the desert relationship to death in his book *Soul Making*:

> Facing death gives our loving force, clarity, and focus ... even our despair is to be given up and seen as the ego-grasping device that it really is. Despair about ourselves and our world is, perhaps, the ego's last and, therefore, greatest attachment. (p. 60)

In the desert tradition, death is a friend and companion along the journey. St. Francis of Assisi referred to death as "sister" in his famous poem "Canticle of Creation." Rather than simply a presence at the end of our lives, death can become a companion along each step, heightening our awareness of life's beauty and calling us toward living more fully. Living with Sister Death calls us to greater freedom and responsibility. Desert is the ultimate lesson in humility and letting go, as Alan Jones describes in *Soul Making*:

> If we sit still and really listen to it, the fact of our own death will come to us with clarity and freshness. Attention to the voice will force us to experience our fragility, futility, and creatureliness. We will be confronted with the emptiness, terror, and formlessness that lies deep within the heart. This is the desert experience of the saints and mystics, and it is also known to psychoanalysis. Such phrases as "the cloud of unknowing" and "the dark night of the soul" are different ways to try to talk about this experience of emptiness. To the believer, this vast inner emptiness is nothing less than the dwelling place of God. (p. 69)

Abba Evagrius said, "Sit in your cell, collecting your thoughts. Remember the day of your death. See then what the death of your body will be; let your spirit be heavy, take pains, condemn the vanity of the world, so as to be able always to live in the peace you have in view without weakening."[21]

(EVAGRIUS 1)

He also said, "Always keep your death in mind...."

(EVAGRIUS 4)

22   One of the goals in the desert way of prayer is *apatheia*, which is a sense of stillness and inner peace. It is a release from being caught up in the demands of our thoughts; it is freedom. *Apatheia* is not apathy, it is a kind of non-attachment to the things that keep us from what should be our one true passion: a radical embrace of love.

Apatheia is similar to what Buddhists call "emptiness." Hinduism speaks of "detachment," the Sufis of "sobriety," and the thirteenth-century Christian mystic Meister Eckhart writes of *Abgescheidenheit,* which means "cutting off." When we can regard our inner life and the world around us without getting hooked into the drama of it, this is *apatheia*. It is a function of our inner witness and being in compassionate presence to what is, rather than being caught up in and over-identifying with the story going on in our thoughts.

This detachment isn't about material goods and possessions. Instead, it is an invitation to transform our inner relationship to our thoughts; it is a spiritual capacity or stance toward life, and it requires continual development or practice.

23   This excerpt is drawn from David G. R. Keller, *Oasis of Wisdom*, p. 30.

The state of prayer can be aptly described as a habitual state of imperturbable calm [apatheia].[22] It snatches to the heights of intelligible reality the spirit which loves wisdom and which is truly spiritualized by the most intense love.... The man who strives after true prayer must learn to master not only anger and his lust, but must free himself from every thought that is colored by passion.

(EVAGRIUS)[23]

[24] This path of unknowing is at the heart of desert spirituality. We release everything we think we know to rest in the source of all truth. We even move toward letting go of our ideas about God. As quoted in Alan Jones's *Soul Making*, Christian mystic Simone Weil tells us that "There are two atheisms of which one is a purification of the notion of God" (p. 9). The call of the desert is to let go, let go, let go, and let go some more, on every level of our lives. The desert has the power to open our hearts to what our minds cannot understand.

John Cassian describes three renunciations he says are required of all of us on the spiritual journey:

> First, we must renounce our former way of life and move closer to our heart's desires, toward the interior life. Second, we must do the inner work (of asceticism) by renouncing our mindless thoughts. This renunciation is particularly difficult because we have little control over our thoughts. Third, and finally, we must renounce our own images of God so that we can enter into contemplation of God as God. (Mary Margaret Funk, *Thoughts Matter* [Continuum, 1999], 9)

The *via negativa* or *apophatic* way in Christian tradition demands that we talk about God only in terms of negatives, in terms of what God is not. This cleanses us of our idols. "We can only say that God is both unknowable and inexhaustible" (Alan Jones, *Soul Making*, 26). Humility is required. We are very attached to our ideas of who God is and how God works in the world. Ultimately, the desert journey demands that we let go of even this false idol in our thoughts and open ourselves to the God who is far more expansive than we can behold or imagine.

One day some old men came to see Abba Anthony. In the midst of them was Abba Joseph. Wanting to test them, the old man suggested a text from the Scriptures, and, beginning with the youngest, he asked them what it meant. Each gave his opinion as he was able. But to each one the old man said, "You have not understood it." Last of all he said to Abba Joseph, "How would you explain this saying?" and he replied, "I do not know." Then Abba Anthony said, "Indeed, Abba Joseph has found the way, for he has said: 'I do not know.'"[24]

(ANTHONY THE GREAT 17)

1 | The desert fathers and mothers counseled that having a wise elder or soul friend was an essential aspect of the spiritual life. This "manifestation of thoughts" is not a form of confession or psychotherapy, and it is not a forced act. It must be offered from a free and willing heart as part of a movement toward greater internal freedom. To share something that feels shameful is to free ourselves from that shame and have it accepted in a compassionate way by a wise other.

The role of the wise elder is to be one who listens to the heart of another in order to assist them with discernment about the motivations and drives that govern their lives. It requires an act of trust to believe that this kind of transparency and humility leads to transformation. Our initial impulse is to hide what feels wounded or broken, especially in spiritual communities.

✳ | The desert concept of the spiritual elder had a significant impact on the early Celtic Church. This is the origin of the idea of an *anamchara* (from the Gaelic), meaning "soul friend"; someone who has acted as a teacher or spiritual guide to another. In the earliest days of the church this role was open to both lay people and the ordained, men and women alike.

In Sellner's *Stories of Celtic Soul Friends*, there is a story of St. Brigit of Kildare reflecting on the importance of the *anamchara*:

> Go forth and eat nothing until you get a soul friend, for anyone
> without a soul friend is like a body without a head; is like the water
> of a polluted lake, neither good for drinking nor for washing. That
> is the person without a soul friend. ([Paulist Press, 2004], 7)

It was their capacity for deep friendship and the ability to read other people's hearts that became the basis of the desert elders' effectiveness as spiritual guides. What the stories about the desert Christians reveal is that, despite their love of solitude, or perhaps precisely because of that love, friendship had a special meaning for them. At the same time, it is clear that these desert guides—revered for their friendship,

(continued on page 86)

☐ Spiritual Elders and Soul Friends

A brother asked Abba Poemen: "Why should I not be free to do without manifesting my thoughts to the old men?"[1] The old man replied: "Abba John the Dwarf said: 'The enemy rejoices over nothing so much as over those who do not manifest their thoughts.'"

(POEMEN 101)

hospitality, and compassion—also valued silence and solitude, even when they lived within monasteries. "The goal of the desert was utter transparence to divine light. The elder, far from being a center of power and a 'director,' served in his or her transparence to divine light as a lens that could focus the light of truth on the dark places in the disciple's heart." See Columba Stewart, "The Desert Fathers on Radical Self-Honesty" (*Vox Benedictina* 8.1 [Summer 1991], 10-11).

The desert elders believed that we cannot truly know our heart or transform our passions without a spiritual guide or counselor. This spiritual director is someone who keeps us honest, someone to whom we become accountable. Without this accountability, it is easy to fool ourselves into thinking we are traveling along the right path when we are not.

2 In its literal sense, the monk counts drops of water as part of the practice of fasting.

✳ When we reveal our thoughts and our deep, dark secrets to a trusted person, this can be an act of healing. We are released from the secrecy and shame of our compulsions. We learn that others struggle in this way, too.

The contemplative path can be a painful experience at times. We are confronted with our own deep wounds and needs. Because of this wounding, we simply can't go this way alone and be our own healer. We need a wise guide, someone who has been immersed in this path themselves and who has journeyed further than we have. As Abba Poemen wisely suggests (see p. 89), we must also be discerning as to whom to give our trust when we are naming our places of weakness. We must find someone who has been through the desert themselves, has sat with their own inner demons, has tasted great loss, someone who can offer us wisdom along the way and support us on the difficult path.

And the point is to reveal our inner thoughts—including, even especially, those thoughts that have been darker and more difficult to manage. There is a call to an unrelenting sense of accountability and responsibility. In this process the elder can help us point out patterns

(continued on page 88)

[Abba Anthony] said this, "If he is able to, a monk ought to tell his elders confidently how many steps he takes and how many drops of water he drinks in his cell,[2] in case he is in error about it."

(ANTHONY 38)

and habits that we are not aware of. The elder can help us to discern our conflicting desires of the heart. This demands vulnerability and humility on our part, which for the desert monks is the path toward transformation.

Logismoi are the thoughts that were considered to be demonic or were derived purely from ego and self-will—attachments to that which stands in opposition to God's desires for us. When the *logismoi* arise, they are attractive to us, and they stir our passions. It can seem like a good idea, for instance, that we consider our commitment to spiritual practice as more important than our relationship to God. This passage is also about priorities and right relationship. Many spiritual writers of the East refer to these thoughts in terms of their "degrees of penetration." There were several stages described, beginning with the suggestion of an impure thought, followed by the consideration of whether to follow through with this thought (should I or shouldn't I?), then comes "mental consent," where we internally assent to whatever this thought is asking of us, and finally is captivity, where we become enslaved by the thought and lose our interior freedom because of our obsession with it. See Mary Forman, *Desert Mothers*, p. 60.

In the desert tradition, the spiritual elders were gifted at helping to root out the origin of thoughts and discerning whether those thoughts were drawing one toward God or away. The *amma* or *abba* was a "witness and encourager"—not trying to control the process, but creating space for the novice to discern themselves. This process of opening oneself up to a soul friend was to draw nearer to God and make a commitment to turn oneself in God's direction. By naming these things aloud we help to strip away the masks, fantasies, and projections. (p. 61)

3 This saying indicates that age is not necessary for wisdom in the desert tradition. The spiritual elder is the one who has journeyed the way of the desert. An elder has committed to the path and speaks from experience and commitment to beginning again and again. In his Rule, Benedict writes that older monks should listen to younger ones, for sometimes wisdom comes from unexpected sources.

He also said, "Do not lay open your conscience to anyone whom you do not trust in your heart."

(POEMEN 201)

Abba Joseph said, "While we were sitting with Abba Poemen he mentioned Agathon as 'abba,' and we said to him, 'He is very young, why do you call him "abba"?' Abba Poemen said, 'Because his speech makes him worthy to be called abba.'"[3]

(POEMEN 61)

4   Fornication in the desert tradition means anything that possesses a person's heart and keeps them from God, so it may include sexuality, but it also encompasses a great deal more. Replacing God with anything is considered idolatry.

5   The monk's cell was sometimes referred to as their cave, since some monks lived in these natural dwellings rather than a human-built structure.

6   There are different levels of significance contained in this story. One is the disciple's willingness to manifest his thoughts to Abba Lot. Another is Abba Lot's willingness to carry half of the repentance for this thought in a loving and compassionate way, giving the disciple a word of hope. There is a beautiful sense of mutual trust happening here.

It was related of a brother who had committed a fault that when he went to Abba Lot, he was troubled and hesitated, going in and coming out, unable to sit down. Abba Lot said to him, "What is the matter brother?" He said, "I have committed a great fault and I cannot acknowledge it to the Fathers." The old man said to him, "Confess it to me, and I will carry it." Then he said to him, "I have fallen into fornication,[4] and in order to do it, I have sacrificed idols." The old man said to him, "Have confidence, repentance is possible. Go, sit in your cave,[5] eat only once in two days and I will carry half your fault with you." After three weeks, the old man had the certainty that God has accepted the brother's repentance. Then the latter remained in submission to the old man until his death.[6]

(LOT 2)

1 *Penthos* are tears of compunction, a puncturing of the hard shell of the heart, which pierces to our core, reminding us of who we most deeply are. This "gift of tears," as they are sometimes referred to, reveals to us the misguided perfectionism, games, and manipulations we struggle to achieve, as well as the stories we tell ourselves. These tears free us from lying and any form of pretense that takes over when we feel anxious. In the Eastern Orthodox tradition, the sacrament of confession is sometimes called the "Mystery of the Second Baptism." The ones who truly confess are baptized again in their own tears, symbolizing the in-breaking of truth and freedom.

Tears are another essential element of the monastic way. Tears of compunction fall when we are awakened to realities that had been, until now, hidden beneath our conscious awareness. Often they are stirred when we deepen our contemplative practice and begin to get in touch with all the ways we have turned away from God and from ourselves. We discover something authentic and meaningful, and grief is unleashed over having ignored it for so long. Compunction comes both through God's grace and our own open-heartedness. Benedict writes in his Rule: "We must know that God regards our purity of heart and tears of compunction, not our many words" (20:3).

✳ You have likely had the experience where you were sitting in silence, and suddenly a great sadness rose up in you, and you weren't certain where it came from. Prayer works through the many layers of our defenses, so that we keep discovering what feels like new levels of grief and sorrow at how far away we have allowed ourselves to wander from the heart.

John Chryssavgis writes: "Tears and weeping indicate a significant frontier in the way of the desert. They bespeak a promise. In fact, they are the only way into the heart" (*In the Heart of the Desert*, 48). This frontier is the boundary between our old way of seeing and believing and the wide new expansiveness into which contemplative prayer calls us. Compunction awakens us to all the ways we have been false to our own deepest self and to the profound longing that is kindled when we pay attention to the heart.

☐ Tears of Compunction

It was said of [Abba Arsenius] that he had a hollow in his chest channeled out by the tears[1] which fell from his eyes all his life while he sat at his manual work. When Abba Poemen learned that he was dead, he said weeping, "Truly you are blessed, Abba Arsenius, for you wept for yourself and this world! He who does not weep for himself here below will weep eternally hereafter; so it is impossible not to weep, either voluntarily or when compelled through suffering."

(ARSENIUS 41)

2 The spirit of controversy is the inner battle we have with ourselves, where different parts of our selves feel in conflict. It is the endless chatter that keeps us from the true stillness the desert elders sought. When we move into time for silent prayer, inevitably these desires, anxieties, and chatter will arise; it is part of the human condition. The key is to not let ourselves be swept away by their power, but to keep returning to the breath and the silence, gently releasing that which does not serve us.

3 Compunction is an interior stance of grace-filled and humble self-knowledge, recognizing that you are always on the journey and have never arrived. It is the combination of two words from the Greek: *penthos* and *katanyxis*, meaning "a sudden shock, an emotion which plants deep in the soul a feeling, an attitude, or a resolution" (Irenee Hausher, *Penthos: The Doctrine of Compunction in the Christian East*, 8).

In the ancient monastic tradition, the connection between these two was understood as a moment in a monk's life when something happened that caused the monk to become deeply aware that he had made a choice to move away from God. Compunction leads to sorrow and a gift of tears. These tears begin as an experience of reconciliation, and then move toward joy and the experience of being received back into the arms of God no matter how far the monk has strayed.

These tears come through a recognition of our own limitations. They are tears of profound honesty with ourselves about the ways we have sabotaged ourselves or hurt the ones we love. Tears of compunction are like a great cleansing river running through the heart of the desert, releasing our sorrow and grief, so that we might return to God free of encumbrance.

A brother said to Abba Moses, "Give me a word." He said to him, "Restrain the spirit of controversy[2] in yourself in everything, and weep, have compunction,[3] for the time is drawing near."

(MATOES 12)

4 | This saying is from Andrew Louf, "Humility and Obedience in the Monastic Tradition" (*Cistercian Studies*, vol. XVIII, [1983:4], 272). Isaac of Niniveh was a seventh-century saint who later became a bishop. He spent many years of his life in a monastery and living in solitude as a hermit in the wilderness of Mount Matout.

※ | The "gift of tears" written about by the desert elders and several centuries later by St. Ignatius of Loyola are not about finding meaning in our pain and suffering. They do not give answers but instead call us to a deep attentiveness to the longings of our heart. They continue to flow until we drop our masks and self-deception and return to the source of our lives and longing. They are a sign that we have crossed a threshold into a profound sense of humility:

> Tears come when we learn to live more and more out of our deepest longings, our needs, our troubles. These must surface and be given their rightful place. For in them we find our real human life in all its depths. And when one begins with these unacceptable feelings and desires, which have to be submitted for examination, we must look closely at, and learn to live with, this amazing degree of weakness of ours. (Andrew Louf, "Humility and Obedience in the Monastic Tradition," *Cistercian Studies*, vol. XVIII, [1983:4], 268)

God is felt in the places of pain and sorrow, in the places of paradox and contradiction. Our tears reveal our deepest joys when we acknowledge that we cannot possess anything, neither the spring blossoming nor our partner in life. We learn to love without holding on, without possessing.

The gift of tears brings with it discomfort and pain that comes when we finally allow ourselves to have a direct experience of reality. They do not arise from fear or compulsion. The opposite of *penthos* is *acedia*, which we have discussed before, and sometimes appears like sorrow but actually rejects the hard work of softening the heart and leads to greater self-centeredness. *Penthos* leads to greater God-centeredness.

(*continued on page 98*)

He who is aware of his sins is greater than one who can raise the dead. Whoever can weep over himself for one hour is greater than the one who is able to teach the whole world; whoever recognizes the depth of his own frailty is greater than the one who sees visions of angels.

(ISAAC OF NINIVEH)[4]

A brother asked Abba Poemen what he should do about his sins. The old man said to him, "He who wishes to purify his faults purifies them with tears and he who wishes to acquire virtues, acquires them with tears; for weeping is the way the Scriptures and our Fathers give us, when they say 'Weep! Truly there is no other way than this.'"

(POEMEN 119)

Tears are agents of resurrection, ushering us into new life—life lived awake and fully present. St. Ephrem writes: "Give God weeping, and increase the tears in your eyes, through your tears and his goodness the soul which has been dead will be restored" (Irene Hausherr, *Penthos: The Doctrine of Compunction in the Christian East* [Cistercian Publication, 1982], 29).

✳ In *Soul Making*, Alan Jones describes saints as those who "have been allowed to see into themselves and have not refused to look" (p.101). This reminds me of David Whyte's provocative question in one of his poems, "The Sun": "Why are we the one terrible part of creation privileged to refuse our own flowering?" (*House of Belonging* [Many Rivers Press, 1997]). The path of brokenness is lined with all the ways we have refused to look at our wounds and all the moments we have refused our own flowering. When we finally awaken to this reality, the proper response, the desert monks tell us, is tears.

5 The capacity to discern between the quality of spirits affecting a person was one of the gifts of the *ammas* and *abbas*. Sadness can be beneficial or it can rise up from a state of depression, feelings of guilt or shame, or *accidie*, which relies on self-effort rather than surrendering to God. Syncletica is distinguishing between these two kinds of grief.

6 With *accidie*, one is tempted to abandon the monastic vocation altogether, and so Syncletica's advice to focus on the very practices that sustain the monastic life—prayer and psalmody (singing the psalms as a form of prayer)—shows great wisdom.

There is a grief that is useful, and there is a grief that is destructive. The first sort consist in weeping over one's own faults and weeping over the weakness of one's neighbors, in order not to destroy one's purpose, and attach oneself to the perfect good. But there is also a grief that comes from the enemy, full of mockery, which some call accidie.[5] This spirit must be cast out, mainly by prayer and psalmody.[6]

(SYNCLETICA 27)

1 Do not be impatient, but deepen into the wisdom already offered here. We are reminded that we already know everything we need in this moment in order to live fully. There is no other book or experience that will make us more complete. Once this has been integrated through practice we will naturally be drawn to seek more. That is the nature of a curious and hungry heart. But again, the caution is to not let the words in a book or of others become a substitute for our own deep knowing.

☐ The Necessity of Practice

A brother came to Abba Theodore and began to converse with him about things which he had never yet put into practice. So the old man said to him, "You have not yet found a ship nor put your cargo aboard it and before you have sailed, you have already arrived at the city. Do the work first; then you will have the speed you are making now."

(THEODORE OF PHERME 9)

Abba Abraham told of a man of Scetis who was a scribe and did not eat bread. A brother came to beg him to copy a book. The old man whose spirit was engaged in contemplation, wrote, omitting some phrases and with no punctuation. The brother, taking the book and wishing to punctuate it, noticed that words were missing. So he said to the old man, "Abba, there are some phrases missing." The old man said to him, "Go, and practice first that which is written,[1] then come back and I will write the rest."

(ABRAHAM 3)

2 This story is in part about stability and keeping our commitment to ongoing practice day after day. The commitment to practice, even without the visible evidence of results, brings us back to the concept of *apatheia*—detachment from the results of our practice. When we continually begin again, the fruit will come with time.

We are also reminded here of *hupomone*, patience, which we explored earlier in this book. Patience isn't just about being comfortable with the slow passage of time, but about coming into a new relationship with time; God's time:

> In eschatological [sic] time each moment is filled with both "what needs to be done" and the inner awareness that God is present in that need and desires its fulfillment.... Time was experienced differently by the desert elders. Chronological time depends on duration. It can impose limitations on the ego when it is associated with completing a goal. It establishes a boundary for expectations and the ego strains to accomplish what it desires. Time accentuates the need for control of what happens within time. This is a major source of anxiety and can lead to despair.... Patience is the resistance to duration. We resist the duration of time, not its passing— time does not demand resistance, seeing that is passes anyway. We resist that which endows time with duration: affliction, waiting, anxiety, and it is precisely in this resistance that the soul is shaped. (David Keller, *Oasis of Wisdom*, 68-69)

When we are waiting for a particular outcome, we are often filled with anxiety as we sit with the unknown. Patience calls us to remember that God's time (which is beyond our chronological time) is present to us in our waiting. We can experience the fullness of time in the midst of waiting for time to unfold.

Practice can feel tedious because we want immediate results. The desert elders remind us to take the long view.

It was said of Abba John the Dwarf that he withdrew and lived in the desert at Scetis with an old man of Thebes. His abba, taking a piece of dry wood, planted it, and said to him, "Water it every day with a bottle of water, until it bears fruit." Now the water was so far away that he had to leave in the evening and return the following morning. At the end of three years the wood came to life and bore fruit. Then the old man took some of the fruit and carried it to the church saying to the brethren, "Take and eat the fruit of obedience."[2]

(JOHN THE DWARF 1)

3   Also known as Epiphanius of Salamis, considered a church father by both the Eastern Orthodox and Catholic churches.

4   Or, "The Little Hours," mean, respectively, "the third hour," "the sixth hour," and "the ninth hour." In antiquity, time was measured by dividing day and night into twelve "hours," the length of which varied from summer to winter. It has been Christian tradition from the earliest centuries to pause for prayer at the third hour of the day (midmorning), at the sixth hour (midday), and at the ninth hour (midafternoon).

✳   The desert monastics lived patterned lives. Not every monk or community lived under the same pattern, but they often had similar elements, and all were focused on cultivating a deep intimacy with the holy presence everywhere and at all times. The pattern of the monks' lives had both internal and external dimensions. The internal aspects were concerned with presence to one's heart and doing battle with the passions that we explored earlier.

The external aspects were concerned with things like prayer, work, meals, and the cell where a monk lived. Depending on whether a monk lived in community or as a hermit, there would be a regular gathering to pray the psalms together in the tradition of the liturgy of the hours. With little access to written texts, the scriptures were often memorized and repeated again and again as a way of integrating the words into the heart, so they could be called upon at any time.

This patterned way of life continued to flourish in the development of later monastic communities. In the Rule of Benedict, there are detailed instructions about praying the Liturgy of the Hours or Fixed Hour Prayer. The monks gathered seven times a day to chant the psalms together. This practice was considered the centerpiece of their lives. When the bell rang for prayer the monk was to drop everything, even if he was right in the midst of important work. In this way, the monks cultivated humility and remembered throughout the day to return their attention to God.

The blessed Epiphanius, Bishop of Cyprus,[3] was told this by the abbot of a monastery which he had in Palestine, "By your prayers we do not neglect our appointed round of psalmody, but we are very careful to recite Terce, Sext and None."[4] Then Epiphanius corrected them with the following comment, "It is clear that you do not trouble about the other hours of the day, if you cease from prayer. The true monk should have prayer and psalmody continually in his heart."

(EPIPHANIUS, BISHOP OF CYPRUS 3)

| 5 | This saying is drawn from Epiphanius, Bishop of Cyprus, 7.

| 6 | Abba Nisterus has us ask two questions each night and morning. I will rephrase them slightly as: "What have I done that is in alignment with God's deepest desire for me?" and "Where have I resisted or said no to that which is not healthy for me?"

The purpose of regular spiritual practice is to continually remind ourselves of who we are and where our focus should be. Gregory Mayers describes this as a process of awakening us in *Listen to the Desert*: "from the affliction of our amnesia to the Truth of our own Original Identity. We have not only forgotten who we are, but we have also forgotten that we have forgotten, settling for the illusion of our forgetful condition. We have forgotten that we are Deus incognito" (pp. 55–56). We have not just fallen asleep, but we have numbed ourselves to this condition of being asleep. Practice is the bell of awakening, offering us the opportunity to remember again and again.

| ✳ | Reading this saying, I am reminded of St. Ignatius of Loyola's prayer of examen, where each night you reflect on your day and ask two questions: What was the most life-giving moment? What was the most life-draining moment? This is a very valuable practice to engage in and keep track over time of what kinds of experiences keep coming up. Using this practice, I have discovered hidden patterns that brought me more joy than I realized as well as situations where I was called to take a stronger stand and say no to something that was draining my energy. The prayer of examen can be an essential tool for discerning life choices.

The same old man said, "David the prophet prayed late at night; waking in the middle of the night, he prayed before the day, at the dawn of the day he stood before the Lord; in the small hours he prayed, in the evening and at mid-day he prayed again, and this is why he said, 'Seven times a day have I praised you.'" (Ps. 119:164)[5]

Abba Nisterus said that a monk ought to ask himself every night and every morning, "What have we done that is as God wills and what have we left undone of that which he does not will?"[6] "He must do this throughout his whole life. This is how Abba Arsenius used to live. Every day strive to come before God without sin. Pray to God for his presence, for he really is present. Do not impose rules on yourself; do not judge anyone. Swearing, making false oaths, lying, getting angry, insulting people laughing, all that is alien to monks, and he who is esteemed or exalted above that which he deserves suffers great harm."

(NISTERUS 5)

7   We can so easily become discouraged in the life of prayer. Practice and discipline may bring to mind running laps around a track or practicing scales on a musical instrument—repetitive, dull, and without immediate gratification. Or, we may simply lose hope that we are capable of a spiritual life at all when we keep falling away from our commitments. This story, as told by an anonymous desert elder, offers the image of the gift of daily practice. The desert monks urge us to show up even for a few minutes, day-by-day.

8   This excerpt is drawn from Rowan Williams, *Silence and Honey Cakes*, p. 88.

A brother fell when he was tempted, and in his distress he stopped practicing his monastic rule. He really longed to take it up again, but his own misery prevented him. He would say to himself, "When shall I be able to be holy in the way I used to be before?"

He went to see one of the old men, and told him all about himself. And when the old man learned of his distress, he said: "There was a man who had a plot of land; but it got neglected and turned into waste ground, full of weeds and brambles. So he said to his son, 'Go and weed the ground.' The son went off to weed it, saw all the brambles and despaired. He said to himself, 'How long will it take before I have uprooted and reclaimed all that?' So he lay down and went to sleep for several days. His father came to see how he was getting on and found he had done nothing at all. 'Why have you done nothing?' he said. The son replied, 'Father, when I started to look at this and saw how many weeds and brambles there were, I was so depressed that I could do nothing but lie down on the ground.'[7] His father said, 'Child, just go over the surface of the plot every day and you will make some progress.' So he did, and before long the whole plot was weeded. The same is true for you, brother: work just a little bit without getting discouraged, and God by his grace will re-establish you."

(ANONYMOUS 76)[8]

1 The desert life was not for its own sake. Retreating to silence, becoming conscious of one's own inner voices, being present to suffering, releasing all that gets in the way of God, all of these are ultimately in service to our growing capacity for love. Their aim was God and charity was the path.

❋ The desert way will always lead us back to others if we are having an authentic experience of God and of our deepest selves. One of the ways we know if our prayer is bearing fruit is to ask: Does my inner work cultivate in me a wider heart and capacity to be present?

The desert fathers and mothers are often described doing works of charity, such as caring for the needs of the sick and staying with them until they are restored. This capacity emerges from their deep core and time spent tending to their inner sanctuary. As it developed through the ages, monastic tradition continued to be associated with hospitality and attending to the needs of others in a variety of ways.

In *Listen to the Desert*, Gregory Mayers describes charity as being "free of the tyranny of the self" (pp. 121–122). As the desert monks moved through their daily lives, they cultivated an ability to let go of their self-consciousness about whether they were doing something correctly and their self-preoccupation about whether their spiritual practice was getting them somewhere. The motivations behind so many of our actions are to be loved, approved of, seen, or accepted. These are all valid needs. However, we get transfixed by them, and they become the primary reason we do anything at all. Those who advanced on the desert path moved slowly past these tiring and narrow concerns about the self, cultivating a wider heart. They were able to step outside of themselves and meet others as they are.

The desert monks knew that detachment from one's own desires created more space and freedom to be available to others. When we recognize that the world does not revolve around our own desires and needs, we discover that we can be a healing presence to others.

☐ Virtues, Charity, and the Service of Love

Abba Agathon said, "If I could meet a leper, give him my body and take his, I should be very happy." That indeed is perfect charity.

It was also said of him that, coming to the town one day to sell his wares, he encountered a sick traveller lying in the public palace without anyone looking after him. The old man rented a cell and lived with him there, working with his hands to pay the rent and spending the rest of the money on the sick man's needs. He stayed there four months till the sick man was restored to health. Then he returned in peace to his cell.[1]

(AGATHON 26–27)

2 In nurturing the contemplative life, the desert elders offer us the gift of the virtues as essential tools in cultivating a meaningful life. The virtues are an ancient ethical tradition in Christianity. Rather than focus on an "acts-based" morality, where we create a list of things we aren't supposed to do, virtue ethics invite us to consider a sense of morality and goodness rooted in relationship, meaning, and the kind of life we want to create. Instead of focusing on all the ways we are tempted away from being present to God, we can foster a way of being that gives us strength and peace through the virtues. This is a positive approach to our habits and behavior, rather than always focusing on what we shouldn't be doing.

3 Abba John the Dwarf suggests that when we experience fear and suffering, we ought to cultivate patience. When we experience distress, we can cultivate humility. When we start to feel angry, we can cultivate peace.

✳ Practice prudence by bringing wisdom to our decisions and refraining from taking unnecessary risks. Practice justice by asking questions about those who have less than we do, looking for root causes of injustice and ways we can respond. Practice courage by considering those places in our lives where we experience fear and self-limitation. Carry a sense of strength to whatever life brings us and a willingness to go into unknown places for the sake of growing closer to God and to our own deep desires.

✳ For me, courage doesn't mean eliminating fear, it means being fully present to the fear, asking what the fear is trying to protect me from, and if the threat isn't a real one, courage gives me the strength to move forward into new possibilities.

✳ We also have another reminder in this story of the nearness of our own death. Remembering our own mortality is also a call to more closely examine how we are living.

Abba John said, "I think it best that a man should have a little bit of all the virtues.[2] Therefore, get up early every day and acquire the beginning of every virtue and every commandment of God. Use great patience, with fear and long-suffering, in the love of God, with all the fervor of your soul and body. Exercise great humility, bear with interior distress, be vigilant and pray often with reverence and groaning, with purity of speech and control of your eyes. When you are despised do not get angry, be at peace, and do not render evil for evil. Do not pay attention to the faults of others, and do not try to compare yourself with others, knowing you are less than every created thing. Renounce everything material and that which is of the flesh. Live by the cross, in warfare, in poverty of spirit, in voluntary spiritual asceticism, in fasting, penitence, and tears, in discernment, in purity of soul, taking hold of that which is good. Do your work in peace. Persevere in keeping vigil, in hunger and thirst, in cold and nakedness, and in sufferings. Shut yourself in a tomb as though you were already dead, so that at all times you will think death is near."[3]

(JOHN THE DWARF 34)

4 Again, we are reminded of the desert elders, fierceness of spiritual life. While the scriptures were revered as sources of profound wisdom, we can hold too tightly to words and what we think they mean. Before we even try to understand what the scriptures teach us, we must first cultivate humility and patience. These virtues are the "beginning of wisdom."

5 Saying CXXXIII is drawn from Thomas Merton's *Wisdom of the Desert*, p. 171, as quoted in the *Verba Seniorum*. These stories were translated from a Latin text and do not have specific names attributed to them.

Two brethren went to an elder who lived alone in Scete. And the first one said: Father, I have learned all of the Old and New Testaments by heart. The elder said to him: You have filled the air with words. The other one said: I have copied out the Old and New Testaments and have them in my cell. And to this one the elder replied: You have filled your window with parchment. But do you now know Him who said: The kingdom of God is not in words, but in power? And again, not those who hear the Law will be justified before God but those who carry it out. They asked him, therefore, what was the way of salvation, and he said to them: The beginning of wisdom is the fear of the Lord, and humility with patience.[4]

(*VERBA SENIORUM*)[5]

6 "Winning" a neighbor isn't about converting others, but instead is about helping to open their hearts to God's healing. If we do so, we win God, too, because we become a vessel and vehicle for someone else to encounter the Divine in new and life-giving ways. We allow the qualities of the sacred to appear through our being, letting go of our preoccupations and anxieties. We are healed in the process as well.

7 This reading is about more than just making sure to smooth things over with others or not go to bed angry. For me, Abba Isaac's words speak to a commitment to doing the hard work of being in relationship. Imagine first the level of consciousness it takes to know when someone else's actions have grieved us and then the action needed to go to that person to address the issue. In addition to these, to also be in such open communication with one another we must be transparent about whether the other has grieved against us.

The times I have been in conflict with someone I love have been moments when I wanted to run in the other direction. I don't want love to be hard; I want it to be an easy space that receives me as I am. And yet, it is easy to love when we feel in harmony with another. So much more challenging it is to continue to love when we feel at odds with the one we love. We are counseled by the desert elders to stay in that place of discomfort, not rush to easy resolutions, not give over our own needs, and yet at the same time try to meet the other in their needs. This is truly hard work. Yet the rewards of deepened intimacy and trust are invaluable.

Abba John the Dwarf said, "A house is not built by beginning at the top and working down. You must begin with the foundations in order to reach the top." They said to him, "What does this saying mean?" He said, "The foundation is our neighbor, whom we must win,⁶ and that is the place to begin. For all the commandments of Christ depend on this one."

(JOHN THE DWARF 39)

Abba Isaac said, "I have never allowed a thought against my brother who has grieved me to enter my cell; I have seen to it that no brother should return to his cell with a thought against me."⁷

(ISAAC, PRIEST OF THE CELLS 9)

1 The silence of the desert elders is called *hesychia*, which means stillness, silence, inner quiet. However, it is much deeper than just an external quiet. As we have read in other stories, a person can live alone and still experience much noise within, and a person can live in the midst of a crowd and have a true sense of stillness in their heart.

There is always a shadow side to silence, the kind of silence that keeps hidden secrets and abuses. Some silences are quite poisonous, as when a person's voice is being silenced or when we silence ourselves out of resentment or anger. There are times when we have engaged silence as a weapon in a relationship and withheld our voice as a way of punishing someone. There is also the silence of hopelessness or giving up, when we feel overwhelmed by life. Or the silence that comes when we feel another has all the answers and our voice doesn't matter.

The desert monks speak not of these unsupportive silences, but instead of a silence that gives life. They urge us to seek a particular quality of silence that is attentive and emerges from a place of calm and peace. Our freedom to be silent in this way indicates our freedom from resentment and its power over us. Authentic silence is very challenging to achieve.

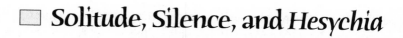 # Solitude, Silence, and *Hesychia*

It was said of Abba Agathon that for three years he lived with a stone in his mouth, until he had learnt to keep silence.[1]

(AGATHON 15)

☀ When we find ourselves releasing words and simply entering into an experience of wonder and beholding, this is the silence of God; these are moments when we are arrested by life's beauty.

Silence is, indeed, challenging. We create all kinds of distractions and noise in our lives so that we can avoid it. Thomas Merton writes about people who go to church and lead good lives yet find this interior silence so hard to achieve:

> Interior solitude is impossible for them. They fear it. They do everything they can to escape it. What is worse, they try to draw everyone else into activities as senseless and as devouring as their own. They are great promoters of useless work. They love to organize meetings and banquets and conferences and lectures. They print circulars, write letters, talk for hours on the telephone in order that they may gather a hundred people together in a large room where they will all fill the air with smoke and make a great deal of noise and roar at one another and clap their hands and stagger home at last patting one another on the back with the assurance that they have all done great things to spread the Kingdom of God. (*New Seeds of Contemplation* [London: Burns & Oates, 1962], 83)

The desert fathers and mothers invite us to consider what it means to be selective with our words. Cultivating silence is about making space for another voice to speak. Silence is a presence rather than an absence. I can fill my day with endless words, or I can choose when to speak and when to keep silent.

2 Sitting in our cell requires patience to not run from ourselves or flee back into the world of distraction and numbness. It means being fully present to our inner life without anxiety. Interior peace comes through sitting in silence, through attentiveness and watchfulness.

A brother asked Abba Rufus, "What is interior peace, and what use is it?" The old man said, "Interior peace means to remain sitting in one's cell with fear and knowledge of God, holding far off the remembrance of wrongs suffered and pride of spirit.[2] Such interior peace brings forth all the virtues, preserves the monk from the burning darts of the enemy, and does not allow him to be wounded by them. Yes, brother, acquire it. Keep in mind your future death, remembering that you do not know at what hour the thief will come. Likewise be watchful over your soul."

(RUFUS 1)

✳ Much of the time I find silence a deep source of consolation. However, there are many times when I find myself wrestling during my silent practice: watching the clock, feeling impatient, restless, and distracted. Tempting thoughts arise: I could get up early and walk away. I am not really present and so should quit and try again tomorrow. And yet the call is precisely to stay with the practice when things become difficult. The desert elders said this was a lifelong struggle. They considered themselves beginners on the spiritual path. I remember this when I struggle to stay put. If these wise elders were beginners, then certainly I have only just begun to explore the possible depths of silence.

The desert elders warn us repeatedly about the ways we resist silence, especially in our interior chatter and the onslaught of thoughts most of us experience when we sit down to pray. In fact, this encounter with silence is often why we resist slowing down and being still. We fear what might be revealed in that space.

3 Regular practice of silent prayer and meditation helps us to grow aware of the chatter of our minds and the judgments we carry about ourselves and others. By becoming fully present to these thoughts and being compassionate with ourselves, we can start to notice when they arise in everyday life. The desert elders remind us to pay attention to our inner judgments; they are a form of noise that poisons the silence we so desperately seek.

Abba Poemen said: "A man may seem to be silent, but if his heart is condemning others he is babbling ceaselessly. But there may be another who talks from morning till night and yet he is truly silent; that is, he says nothing that is not profitable."[3]

(POEMEN 27)

1 See chapter 2, note 7.

✳ As we read through these sayings, we find several variations of "the three essential things" we must do in life. I love that they come in threes, as three is a number that helps us break through dualities. We tend to view life in either/or, us/them, or black/white dichotomies. When a third possibility enters, we are invited to hold the complexity and mystery of life and realize that it is so much vaster than any dichotomous situation. Franciscan priest Richard Rohr describes this as the "third eye" of the mystics, which moves us into non-dualistic thinking. See *The Naked Now: Learning to See as the Mystics See* (New York: Crossroad Publishing Co, 2009), 98–100.

☐ Three Essential Things

Someone asked Abba Anthony, "What must one do in order to please God?" The old man replied, "Pay attention to what I tell you: whoever you may be, always have God before your eyes; whatever you do, do it according to the testament of the holy scriptures; in whatever place you live, do not easily leave it. Keep these three precepts and you will be saved."

(ANTHONY 3)

Abba Andrew said, "These three things are appropriate for a monk: exile, poverty, and endurance in silence."

(ANDREW 37)

As he was dying, Abba Benjamin said to his sons,[1] "If you observe the following, you can be saved, 'Be joyful at all times, pray without ceasing, and give thanks for all things.'"

(BENJAMIN 4)

✳ None of the monks say the same three things. Does this mean that
one is right and the others are wrong? Or does it open us up to the
possibility that the ground can shift beneath us during our lives, and
what feels essential during one season becomes less important in
another?

The desert elders do not offer a systematic, ten-step program for
living a life in the presence of God. Each monk speaks from his or her
own experience, each offers the wisdom earned from years of practice.
There are many dominant themes that we have been exploring in this
book. Even in these particular sayings you will notice some common-
alities between them. But essentially, the stories they tell point to the
need to stay committed to our own truth in this moment, with the
guidance of wise elders, and to see past the dualisms we worship.

Abba Gregory said, "These three things God requires of all the baptized: right faith in the heart, truth on the tongue, temperance in the body."

(GREGORY THE THEOLOGIAN 1)

A brother who followed the life of stillness in the monastery of the cave of Abba Saba came to Abba Elias and said to him, "Abba, give me a way of life." The old man said to the brother, "In the days of our predecessors they took great care about these three virtues: poverty, obedience, and fasting. But among monks nowadays avarice, self-confidence, and great greed have taken charge. Choose whichever you want most."

(ELIAS 8)

Abba Poemen said, "Life in the monastery demands three things: the first is humility, the next is obedience, and the third which sets them in motion is like a goad in the work of the monastery."

(POEMEN 103)

1 In the desert tradition, prayer was focused on letting go and renouncing anything that gets in the way of a relationship with God. Prayer was an acceptance of our own frailty and the frailty of the world we live in.

2 Macarius reminds us that prayer does not need to be complicated or filled with important words. All we need to do is extend ourselves bodily and ask for assistance along the way.

The beauty of the desert monks is that prayer was described differently by each monk, according to their gifts. This was an extraordinarily gracious way to be with the differences we find among people.

☐ Prayer and Differing Gifts

Abba Macarius was asked, "How should one pray?"[1] The old man said, "There is no need at all to make long discourses; it is enough to stretch one's hands and say, 'Lord, as you will, and as you know, have mercy.' And if the conflict grows fiercer say, 'Lord, help!' He knows very well what we need and he shows us his mercy."[2]

(MACARIUS 19)

3 Euchites were fanatics who came to Syria in the late fourth century and professed to give themselves entirely to prayer, refusing to work, and living by begging. Euchites differed from the Christian monks, who supported themselves by their labor.

4 Prayer was a continuous way of life in the desert. Paul's command to "pray without ceasing" formed the foundation of their relationship to prayer; however, how this was interpreted varied. Abba Lucius reminds his visitors that everything is prayer and we can bring our attentiveness to God in all the things that we do. He helps them move past the limited frameworks they have imposed on themselves.

Laura Swan describes the prayer of the desert monks like this:

> Prayer was a continuous way of life in the desert. It was intention-ally cultivated until it became second nature. Prayer involved the hard work of learning a new language—the language of heaven. For the ascetic, prayer was not merely the speaking of words. It was the heart yearning for God, reaching out in hopeful openness to being touched by God. Prayer was for the Holy Spirit breathing through the inner spirit of the ascetic and returning to God with yearnings of intimacy. (Laura Swan, *The Forgotten Desert Mothers: Sayings, Lives, and Stories of Early Christian Women* [Paulist Press, 2001], 27)

Prayer arose directly from the heart, cultivating congruence and integrity. The focus was not on a certain kind of speech, but on the direction of one's longings and gaze. The heart is drawn toward God, and the experience of intimacy in prayer is the fullness of that prayer. The desert fathers and mothers believed that prayer could be experienced at every moment, whereas the Euchites created divisions.

Some of the monks who are called Euchites[3] went to Enaton to see Abba Lucius. The old man asked them, "What is your manual work?" They said, "We do not touch manual work but as the Apostle says, we pray without ceasing." The old man asked them if they did not eat and they replied they did. So he said to them, "When you are eating, who prays for you then?" Again he asked them if they did not sleep and they replied that they did. And he said to them, "When you are asleep, who prays for you then?" They could not find any answer to give him. He said to them, "Forgive me, but you do not act as you speak. I will show you how, while doing my manual work, I pray without interruption. I sit down with God, soaking my reeds and plaiting my ropes, and I say, 'God, have mercy on me, according to the multitude of your mercies, save me from my sins.'" So he asked them if this were not prayer and they replied it was. Then he said to them, "So when I have spent the whole day working and praying, making thirteen pieces of money more or less, I put two pieces of money outside the door and I pay for my food with the rest of the money. He who takes the two pieces of money prays for me when I am eating and when I am sleeping; so; by the grace of God, I fulfill the precept to pray without ceasing."[4]

(LUCIUS 1)

5 Here is a third story with advice on how to pray. This one also speaks to the need to pray depending on one's life circumstances. Interior peace, gratitude, and service with pure intentions are all equivalent paths. None of them can be said to be more exalted.

6 I adore trees and have been known to fall in love with particular ones. They embody such beauty and strength—rooted deep in the earth and reaching toward the heavens. I am struck by the fact that trees need a solid root structure to be able to stretch out their arms. It is the same with us; we each need a solid rooting in the earth to be able to offer our gifts in service to others. This rooting comes in the form of physical nourishment, play, friendship, and spiritual practice.

When I was traveling in Ireland I discovered Ogham, which is an early medieval alphabet appearing often carved into stones. Each letter is based on a different kind of tree, including birch, alder, willow, oak, and hazel. The ancient druids considered trees to be sacred and much of Celtic spirituality celebrates an intimate communion with the natural world. Trees offer wisdom in many ways.

Abba John tells us that the saints are like different trees, each bearing different fruit, but nourished from the same source. And so it is with us as well. When we allow our roots to grow deep, we discover the same source is nourishing each of us. That nourishment gives all of us the strength and courage to bring our gifts to the world, but the fruit we bring will be our own.

7 The desert elders are extraordinarily flexible when it comes to how we live out our calling in the world. The purpose is to do what "your soul desires according to God," which can be hard to discern.

8 The second part of this phrase, "guard your heart," suggests we remain attentive and aware of the competing thoughts and judgments we hold. Notice if a certain path is appealing to us because of some ego boost it promises. Any way of praying is good, as long as the intention is to grow in relationship with God.

Abba Poemen said, "If three men meet, of whom the first fully preserves interior peace, and the second gives thanks to God in illness, and the third serves with a pure mind, these three are doing the same work."[5]

(POEMEN 29)

Abba Poemen said that Abba John said that the saints are like a group of trees, each bearing different fruit but watered from the same source.[6] The practices of one saint differ from those of another, but it is the same Spirit that works in all of them.

(JOHN THE DWARF 43)

A brother questioned an old man saying, "What good work should I do so that I may live?" The old man said, "God knows what is good. I have heard it said that one of the fathers asked Abba Nisterus the Great, the friend of Abba Anthony, and said to him, 'What good work is there that I could do?' He said to him, 'Are not all actions equal? Scripture says that Abraham was hospitable and God was with him. David was humble, and God was with him. Elias loved interior peace and God was with him. So, do whatever you see your soul desires according to God[7] and guard your heart.'"[8]

(NISTERUS 2)

134 Desert Fathers and Mothers

9 In this story we see the confusion of the brother over different priorities. What the saying reveals is the distinctiveness of vocations. Each person has his or her own calling and gifts. Silence and honey cakes need not be in competition with one another. We can each live out the monk's life in the way that reflects our gifts.

It was told of a brother who came to see Abba Arsenius at Scetis that, when he came to the church, he asked the clergy if he could visit Abba Arsenius. They said to him, "Brother, have a little refreshment and then go and see him." "I shall not eat anything," said he, "till I have met him." So, because Arsenius' cell was far away, they sent a brother with him. Having knocked on the door, they entered, greeted the old man and sat down without saying anything. Then the brother from the church said, "I will leave you. Pray for me." Now the visiting brother, not feeling at ease with the old man, said, "I will come with you," and they went away together. Then the visitor asked, "Take me to Abba Moses, who used to be a robber." When they arrived the Abba welcomed them joyfully and then took leave of them with delight. The brother who had brought the other one said to his companion, "See, I have taken you to the foreigner and to the Egyptian, which of the two do you prefer?" "As for me," he replied, "I prefer the Egyptian." Now a father who heard this prayed to God saying, "Lord, explain this matter to me: for Thy name's sake the one flees from men, and the other, for Thy name's sake, receives them with open arms." Then two large boats were shown to him on a river and he saw Abba Arsenius and the Spirit of God sailing in the one, in perfect peace, and in the other was Abba Moses with the angels of God, and they were all eating honey cakes.[9]

(ARSENIUS 38)

1 To become a monk, say the desert elders, we must always be asking the question, "Who am I?" The psychologist Carl Jung said that to lighten the collective shadow, we must do our own inner work. The desert monks offer us invaluable wisdom to do this deep inner work and continue to reflect on the questions of who we are at our deepest core.

2 Our judgments of others often arise because of something within ourselves that we reject. Often when we become aware of these patterns of judgment we discover something of our own self-limits. Desert spirituality calls us to a place of radical solitude and barrenness as a way of stripping away our judgments and all the things that get in the way of self-knowledge.

3 The monk is "toil." This sounds foreboding. Toil is the constant commitment to inner work, to being with thoughts, to battling passions. The Greek word for toil is *kopos* and is considered a desert virtue. We are reminded here that the work of the desert is challenging. We will be tempted again and again to abandon the path. And yet, this is what the monk commits to, the hard work of inner transformation.

4 Abba Lot asks Abba Joseph what more can he do beyond fasting and praying. The response Lot receives is that he can become "consuming fire" and "all flame." The desert elders remind us that there is more to the spiritual life than our commitment to practice. We must allow ourselves to be transformed. We must bring a burning passion to all that we do. We have to allow our times of prayer to fuel our commitment to inner peace and peace in the world. As we sit in threshold places, we can allow the fire to keep us from falling asleep during the time of waiting.

5 Becoming fire is a metaphor for being fully awake. The desert elders call us to always awaken to what is true, to always remember what is holy. This is a story about conversion, about the commitment to ongoing transformation. Conversion later became one of the vows that Benedictine monks would take.

CONCLUSION

☐ How to Become a Monk

Abba Poemen said to Abba Joseph, "Tell me how to become a monk." He said, "If you want to find rest here below, and hereafter, in all circumstances say, Who am I?[1] and do not judge anyone."[2]

(JOSEPH OF PANEPHYSIS 2)

One of the fathers asked Abba John the Dwarf, "What is a monk?" He said, "He is toil.[3] The monk toils at all he does. That is what a monk is."

(JOHN THE DWARF 37)

Abba Joseph said to Abba Lot, "You cannot be a monk unless you become like a consuming fire."[4]

Abba Lot went to see Abba Joseph and said to him, "Abba, as far as I can say my little office, I fast a little, I pray and meditate, I live in peace and as far as I can, I purify my thoughts. What else can I do?" Then the old man stood up and stretched his hands towards heaven. His fingers became like ten lamps of fire and he said to him, "If you will, you can become all flame."[5]

(JOSEPH OF PANEPHYSIS 6–7)

| 6 | You may stop and stumble a bit over this saying. I know I did. The monk who thinks he is an outcast is happy? If the monk's path being toil wasn't enough, then perhaps you are starting to wonder what you got yourself into entering this desert path.

In my book *The Artist's Rule*, I present the monk and artist as archetypes; that is, they each have an energetic presence within them that has been present to people across time and culture. I describe the inner monk as the aspect of us that seeks out a whole-hearted connection to God and cultivates the ability to see the sacred presence shimmering everywhere.

The inner artist seeks to give form to inner longings and create beauty in the world. Both the inner monk and inner artist are border dwellers. Neither fit neatly into mainstream society, and both call us to new ways of being and seeing.

The monk calls the world to spaciousness and presence rather than rushing and productivity. While the world constantly offers possible ways to numb us from everyday struggles, the monk takes the hard and demanding path of inner work and growth. The monk chooses a simple life in the midst of an abundance of riches. When we commit to a contemplative path, we begin to let go of the things that aren't important; we release the non-essentials of life (which society keeps trying to sell us).

To be an outcast means that we don't align ourselves with the dominant way of thinking. It means we live on the lush and fertile edges of life (which paradoxically is also right at the heart and center of things). Think of the incredible richness found in tide pools—that border space between land and sea.

And so, we might find ourselves in a place of deep peace and joy at not "fitting in" anymore, of being essentially an outcast in the world. We might experience a sense of delight that our ways are not the world's ways, but a path rooted in a deeper kind of wisdom.

Living on the borders can also be a lonely place, which is why finding fellow pilgrims is so important. The desert elders speak to us across time. Having soul friends in our lives keeps us grounded and supported.

[Abba Nilus] said, "Happy is the monk who thinks he is the outcast of all."[6]

(NILUS 8)

7 The desert way did not allow much time or space for leisure, but some of the desert fathers and mothers were more balanced in their approach to life and encouraged enjoyment and rest when needed.

❋ While the desert fathers and mothers write extensively about diligence and discipline in the spiritual life, there are also some wonderful stories that remind us about the need to give rest to the body and soul. We live in a world that wants us to shoot arrows from our bow again and again, without regard for how stretched we feel or how close to breaking we often come with the multiplicity of demands placed upon us.

The monk in the world stays committed to the contemplative way through regular practice, but part of that practice is creating spacious-ness and joy. We can allow these desert practices to become another form of competition and productivity, measuring our self-worth by how often or how well we do them. Or we can remember that ultimately it is about something much bigger than ourselves. Sometimes we can only remember the grace available to us when we let go of all of our doing, and rest into our being.

❋ We fool ourselves so easily into believing in the scarcity of things. We crave more and more because we don't believe that we have enough or are enough. The desert elders saw this as the demons at work in our thoughts, making us believe in illusions. In these moments we may find ourselves grasping, greedily hoarding whatever it is we feel the lack of in our lives. To receive, we need to surrender and relinquish; to experience fullness we need to sit with our emptiness. And if we are fortunate, we will remember that the world does not work the way we expect.

In David Keller's *Oasis of Wisdom*, St. John Chrysostom is quoted as saying:

> When Christ orders us to follow the narrow path, he addresses himself to all. The monastic and the lay person must attain the same heights.... Those who live in the world, even though married, ought to resemble the monks in everything else. You are entirely

(continued on page 142)

A hunter in the desert saw Abba Anthony enjoying himself with the brethren[7] and he was shocked. Wanting to show him that it was necessary sometimes to meet the needs of the brethren, the old man said to him, "Put an arrow in your bow and shoot it." So he did. The old man said, "Shoot another," and he did so. Then the old man said, "Shoot yet again," and the hunter replied "If I bend my bow so much I will break it." Then the old man said to him, "It is the same with the work of God. If we stretch the brethren beyond measure they will soon break. Sometimes it is necessary to come down to meet their needs." When he heard these words the hunter was pierced with compunction and, greatly edified by the old man, he went away. As for the brethren, they went home strengthened.

(ANTHONY 13)

mistaken if you think there are some things required of ordinary people, and others of monks. (p. xx)

There is no distinction between the path of the monk living in the desert and the monk living in the city. This path we have been exploring is for everyone. We are each called to it no matter what our life circumstances.

Whether we live in a monastery or not, we can each make the commitment to inner awakening and attentiveness. We each struggle with the hold our thoughts have on our lives, and we seek ways to free them. We each long for the deep peace of *hesychia* to meet us in our daily lives.

8 The more we participate in the sacred feast, the more it expands our hearts. The words we draw upon from scripture to remember these gifts are like a fountain flowing. We need only ask for a "word of guidance and comfort" and we receive a whole book in return.

✳ The desert fathers and mothers recognized that it takes a long time to fully become a human being. It requires patient waiting to re-integrate all the variegated parts of the human heart.

Eventually, through a long and rigorous journey, we might discover that there is indeed blooming that can happen in the desert:

> The wilderness and the dry land shall be glad,
>
> the desert shall rejoice and blossom;
>
> like the crocus it shall blossom abundantly,
>
> and rejoice with joy and singing.

—Isaiah 35:1–2

For Abba Arsenius, this was a rule for the whole of life: "Be solitary, be silent, and be at peace" (*Sayings of the Desert Fathers*, xxi).

I leave you with those three words: solitude, silence, peace. How might you make space for each of those wherever you find yourself?

While yet a child, Abba Ephrem had a dream and then a vision. A branch of vine came out of his tongue, grew bigger and filled everything under heaven. It was laden with beautiful fruit. All the birds of heaven came to eat the fruit of the vine, and the more they ate, the more the fruit increased.[8]

Another time, one of the saints had a vision. According to the commandment of God, a band of angels descended from heaven, holding in their hands a kephalis (that is to say, a piece of papyrus covered with writing), and they said to one another, "To whom should we give this?" Some said, "To this one," others, "To that one." Then the answer came in these words, "Truly, they are holy and righteous, but none of them is able to receive this, except Ephrem." The old man saw that the kephalis was given to Ephrem and he saw as it were a fountain flowing from his lips. Then he understood that which came from the lips of Ephrem was of the Holy Spirit.

(EPHREM 1–2)

Notes ☐

Introduction

1. John Keats, *The Letters of John Keats:* volume 2, 1819–1821 (Cambridge: Cambridge University Press, 2012).

2. "Simplifying the Soul: A Q&A with Paula Huston," by Deborah Arca, *Patheos.com*, January 16, 2012, http://www.patheos.com/Resources/ Additional-Resources/Simplifying-the-Soul-Author-QA-Deborah-Arca-01-16-2012.html.

3. Alan Jones, *Soul Making: The Desert Way of Spirituality* (San Francisco: HarperOne, 1989), 6.

4. Belden C. Lane, *The Solace of Fierce Landscapes: Exploring Desert and Mountain Spirituality* (New York: Oxford University Press, 1998), 20.

5. Alan Jones, *Soul Making*, 6.

6. John Chryssavgis, *In the Heart of the Desert: The Spirituality of the Desert Fathers and Mothers* (Bloomington, IN: World Wisdom, 2003), 76.

7. Timothy Fry, trans., *RB 1980: Rule of St. Benedict in English*, (Collegeville, MN: Liturgical Press, 1982).

8. Andrew Harvey, *A Journey in Ladakh: Encounters with Buddhism* (New York: Houghton Mifflin Harcourt, 2000), 93.

9. Kerry Walters, *Soul Wilderness: A Desert Spirituality* (Mahwah, NJ: Paulist Press, 2001), 59.

10. Gregory Mayers, *Listen to the Desert: Secrets of Spiritual Maturity from the Desert Fathers and Mothers* (Liguori Publications/Triumph Books, 1996), 5.

11. Later on, as Celtic monasticism developed in Ireland, the Celtic monks claimed a similar kind of path that they called "green martyrdom." Since Ireland doesn't have any deserts, the monks wandered out into the wilderness to find solitude and silence. The island of Skellig Michael, off the west coast of Ireland, holds the ruins of a monastic community that formed on this hard-to-reach, tiny hill jutting out of the sea.

12. David G. R. Keller, *Oasis Of Wisdom: The Worlds of the Desert Fathers and Mothers* (Collegeville, MN: Liturgical Press, 2005), 4.

13. Mary Forman, *Praying with the Desert Mothers* (Collegeville, MN: Liturgical Press, 2005), 33.

14. Athanasius, *Life of St. Antony* and Letter to Marcellinius, translated by Robert C. Gregg (Paulist Press: 1979), 33. PLEASE NOTE: The spelling of Anthony's name is without the "h" in this book of his life, but includes the "h" in the sayings texts from Ward.

15. Mary Forman, *Desert Mothers*, 43.

16. Ibid., 41.

17. Derwas James Chitty, *The Desert a City: An Introduction to the Study of Egyptian and Palestinian Monasticism Under the Christian Empire* (Yonkers, NY: St. Vladimirs Seminary Press, 1977).

18. Patricia Wittenberg, *The Rise and Decline of Catholic Religious Orders: A Social Movement Perspective* (Albany: SUNY Press, 1994), 32–33.

19. Mary Forman, *Desert Mothers*, 11.

20. Ibid., 32.

21. This saying is quoted in Mary Forman, *Prayers of the Desert Mothers*, p. 98, and is from John Moschus, *Pratum Sprituale,* 204, PG 87, 3:3093–095.

22. John Chryssavgis, *In the Heart of the Desert*, 22.

23. Ibid., 4.

24. *The World of the Desert Fathers: Stories and Sayings from the Anonymous Series of The Apophthegmata Patrum,* trans. Columba Stewart, (Oxford, UK: SLG Press, 1986). These are sayings for which we have no attribution.

25. Thomas Merton, *The Wisdom of the Desert* (Boston: Shambhala, 2004). These sayings come from a text known as the *Verba Seniorum*, a Latin phrase meaning "words of the elders"; they do not have individual names attributed to them. The sayings were compiled by an anonymous Greek scholar and translated into Latin by Pelagius the Deacon and John the Subdeacon.

26. John Chryssavgis, *The Reflections of Abba Zosimas: Monk of the Palestinian Desert* (Oxford, UK: SLG Press, 2004), XII b.

27. Wayne Teasdale, *A Monk in the World: Cultivating a Spiritual Life* (Novato, CA: New World Library, 2003).

28. Belden C. Lane, *Solace of Fierce Landscapes*, 35.

29. For more information on the practice of *lectio divina*, see my book *Lectio Divina—The Sacred Art: Transforming Words and Images into Heart-Centered Prayer* (Woodstock, VT: SkyLight Paths Publishing, 2011).

30. *The Sayings of the Desert Fathers: The Alphabetical Collection*, trans. Benedicta Ward (Collegeville, MN: Cistercian Publications, 1975), xvi.

Suggestions for Further Reading □

Bourgeault, Cynthia. *The Wisdom Way of Knowing: Reclaiming an Ancient Tradition to Awaken the Heart*. San Francisco: Jossey-Bass, 2003.

Burton-Christie, Douglas. *The Word in the Desert: Scripture and the Quest for Holiness in Early Christian Monasticism*. New York: Oxford University Press, 1993.

Casey, Michael. *A Guide to Living in the Truth: Saint Benedict's Teaching on Humility*. Liguori, MO: Liguori Publications/Triumph Books, 2001.

Chitty, Derwas J. *The Desert a City: An Introduction to the Study of Egyptian and Palestinian Monasticism Under the Christian Empire*. Hoboken, NJ: Blackwell Publishing, 1966.

Chryssavgis, John. *In the Heart of the Desert: The Spirituality of the Desert Fathers and Mothers*. Bloomington, IN: World Wisdom, Inc., 2003.

Chryssavgis, John, trans. *The Reflections of Abba Zosimas: Monk of the Palestinian Desert*. Oxford, UK: SLG Press, 2004, XII b.

Earle, Mary. *The Desert Mothers: Spiritual Practices from the Women of the Wilderness*. New York: Morehouse, 2007.

Forman, Mary. *Praying with the Desert Mothers*. Collegeville, MN: Liturgical Press, 2005.

Funk, Mary Margaret. *Thoughts Matter: The Practice of the Spiritual Life*. New York: Continuum, 1999.

Harmless, William, SJ. *Desert Christians: An Introduction to the Literature of Early Monasticism*. New York: Oxford University Press, 2004.

Jones, Alan. *Soul Making: The Desert Way of Spirituality*. San Francisco: HarperOne, 1989.

Keller, David G. R. *Oasis Of Wisdom: The Worlds of the Desert Fathers and Mothers*. Collegeville, MN: Liturgical Press, 2005.

Lane, Belden C. *The Solace of Fierce Landscapes: Exploring Desert and Mountain Spirituality*. New York: Oxford University Press, 1998.

Mayers, Gregory. *Listen to the Desert: Secrets of Spiritual Maturity from the Desert Fathers and Mothers*. Liguori, MO: Liguori Publications/Triumph Books, 1996.

Merton, Thomas. *New Seeds of Contemplation*. New York: New Directions Publishing, 1961.

———. *The Wisdom of the Desert: Sayings from the Desert Fathers of the Fourth Century*. Boston: Shambhala, 2004.

Norris, Kathleen. *Acedia & Me: A Marriage, Monk's, and A Writer's Life*. New York: Penguin, 2008.

Sellner, Edward C. *Stories of Celtic Soul Friends: Their Meaning for Today*. Mahwah, NJ: Paulist Press, 2004

Stewart, Columba, trans. *The World of the Desert Fathers: Stories and Sayings Form the Anonymous Series of the Apophthegmata Patrum*. Collegeville, MN: Cistercian Publications, 1997.

Swan, Laura. *The Forgotten Desert Mothers: Sayings, Lives, and Stories of Early Christian Women*. New York: Paulist Press, 2001.

Valters Paintner, Christine. Lectio Divina—*The Sacred Art: Transforming Words and Images into Heart-Centered Prayer*. Woodstock, VT: SkyLight Paths, 2011.

Walters, Kerry. *Soul Wilderness: A Desert Spirituality*. Mahwah, NJ: Paulist Press, 2001.

Ward, Benedicta, trans. *The Sayings of the Desert Fathers: The Alphabetical Collection*. Collegeville, MN: Cistercian Publications, 1975.

Williams, Rowan. *Silence and Honey Cakes: The Wisdom of the Desert*. Oxford, UK: Lion Hudson, 2003.

Inspiration

The Golden Rule and the Games People Play
The Ultimate Strategy for a Meaning-Filled Life
By Rami Shapiro
A guidebook for living a meaning-filled life—using the strategies of game theory and the wisdom of the Golden Rule.
6 x 9, 176 pp, Quality PB, 978-1-59473-598-1 **$16.99**

Deepening Engagement
Essential Wisdom for Listening and Leading with Purpose, Meaning and Joy
By Diane M. Millis, PhD; Foreword by Rob Lehman
A toolkit for community building as well as a resource for personal growth and small group enrichment.
5 x 7¼, 176 pp, Quality PB, 978-1-59473-584-4 **$14.99**

The Rebirthing of God
Christianity's Struggle for New Beginnings
By John Philip Newell
Drawing on modern prophets from East and West, and using the holy island of Iona as an icon of new beginnings, Newell dares us to imagine a new birth from deep within Christianity, a fresh stirring of the Spirit.
6 x 9, 160 pp, HC, 978-1-59473-542-4 **$19.99**

Finding God Beyond Religion: A Guide for Skeptics, Agnostics & Unorthodox Believers Inside & Outside the Church
By Tom Stella; Foreword by The Rev. Canon Marianne Wells Borg
Reinterprets traditional religious teachings central to the Christian faith for people who have outgrown the beliefs and devotional practices that once made sense to them. 6 x 9, 160 pp, Quality PB, 978-1-59473-485-4 **$16.99**

Fully Awake and Truly Alive: Spiritual Practices to Nurture Your Soul
By Rev. Jane E. Vennard; Foreword by Rami Shapiro
Illustrates the joys and frustrations of spiritual practice across religious traditions; provides exercises and meditations to help you become more fully alive.
6 x 9, 208 pp, Quality PB, 978-1-59473-473-1 **$16.99**

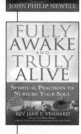

Perennial Wisdom for the Spiritually Independent
Sacred Teachings—Annotated & Explained
Annotation by Rami Shapiro; Foreword by Richard Rohr
Weaves sacred texts and teachings from the world's major religions into a coherent exploration of the five core questions at the heart of every religion's search.
5½ x 8½, 336 pp, Quality PB, 978-1-59473-515-8 **$16.99**

Journeys of Simplicity: Traveling Light with Thomas Merton, Bashō, Edward Abbey, Annie Dillard & Others *By Philip Harnden*
5 x 7¼, 144 pp, Quality PB, 978-1-59473-181-5 **$12.99**

Saving Civility: 52 Ways to Tame Rude, Crude & Attitude for a Polite Planet
By Sara Hacala 6 x 9, 240 pp, Quality PB, 978-1-59473-314-7 **$16.99**

Spiritually Healthy Divorce: Navigating Disruption with Insight & Hope
By Carolyne Call 6 x 9, 224 pp, Quality PB, 978-1-59473-288-1 **$16.99**

Bible Stories / Folktales

Abraham's Bind & Other Bible Tales of Trickery, Folly, Mercy and Love By Michael J. Caduto
New retellings of episodes in the lives of familiar biblical characters explore relevant life lessons. 6 x 9, 224 pp, HC, 978-1-59473-186-0 **$19.99**

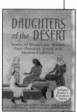

Daughters of the Desert: Stories of Remarkable Women from Christian, Jewish and Muslim Traditions By Claire Rudolf Murphy,
Meghan Nuttall Sayres, Mary Cronk Farrell, Sarah Conover and Betsy Wharton
Breathes new life into the old tales of our female ancestors in faith. Uses traditional scriptural passages as starting points, then with vivid detail fills in historical context and place. Chapters reveal the voices of Sarah, Hagar, Huldah, Esther, Salome, Mary Magdalene, Lydia, Khadija, Fatima and many more. Historical fiction ideal for readers of all ages.
5½ x 8½, 192 pp, Quality PB, 978-1-59473-106-8 **$18.99** Inc. reader's discussion guide

The Triumph of Eve & Other Subversive Bible Tales
By Matt Biers-Ariel These engaging retellings of familiar Bible stories are witty, often hilarious and always profound. They invite you to grapple with questions and issues that are often hidden in the original texts.
5½ x 8½, 192 pp, Quality PB, 978-1-59473-176-1 **$14.99**

Also available: **The Triumph of Eve Teacher's Guide**
8½ x 11, 44 pp, PB, 978-1-59473-152-5 **$8.99**

Religious Etiquette / Reference

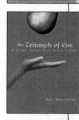

How to Be a Perfect Stranger, 6th Edition: The Essential Religious Etiquette Handbook *Edited by Stuart M. Matlins and Arthur J. Magida*
The indispensable guidebook to help the well-meaning guest when visiting other people's religious ceremonies. A straightforward guide to the rituals and celebrations of the major religions and denominations in the United States and Canada from the perspective of an interested guest of any other faith, based on information obtained from authorities of each religion. Belongs in every living room, library and office. Covers:

African American Methodist Churches • Assemblies of God • Bahá'í Faith • Baptist • Buddhist • Christian Church (Disciples of Christ) • Christian Science (Church of Christ, Scientist) • Churches of Christ • Episcopalian and Anglican • Hindu • Islam • Jehovah's Witnesses • Jewish • Lutheran • Mennonite/Amish • Methodist • Mormon (Church of Jesus Christ of Latter-day Saints) • Native American/First Nations • Orthodox Churches • Pentecostal Church of God • Presbyterian • Quaker (Religious Society of Friends) • Reformed Church in America/Canada • Roman Catholic • Seventh-day Adventist • Sikh • Unitarian Universalist • United Church of Canada • United Church of Christ

"The things Miss Manners forgot to tell us about religion."
                                                        —*Los Angeles Times*

"Finally, for those inclined to undertake their own spiritual journeys … tells visitors what to expect."   —*New York Times*

6 x 9, 416 pp, Quality PB, 978-1-59473-593-6 **$19.99**

Struggling in Good Faith
LGBTQI Inclusion from 13 American Religious Perspectives
Edited by Mychal Copeland and D'vorah Rose; Foreword by Bishop Gene Robinson
A multifaceted sourcebook telling the story of reconciliation, celebration and struggle for LGBTQI inclusion across the religious landscape in America.
6 x 9, 250 pp (est), Quality PB, 978-1-59473-602-5 **$19.99**

The Perfect Stranger's Guide to Funerals and Grieving Practices
A Guide to Etiquette in Other People's Religious Ceremonies
Edited by Stuart M. Matlins 6 x 9, 240 pp, Quality PB, 978-1-893361-20-1 **$16.95**

The Perfect Stranger's Guide to Wedding Ceremonies
A Guide to Etiquette in Other People's Religious Ceremonies
Edited by Stuart M. Matlins 6 x 9, 208 pp, Quality PB, 978-1-893361-19-5 **$16.95**

Sacred Texts—SkyLight Illuminations Series

Offers today's spiritual seeker an enjoyable entry into the great classic texts of the world's spiritual traditions. Each classic is presented in an accessible translation, with facing pages of guided commentary from experts, giving you the keys you need to understand the history, context and meaning of the text.

CHRISTIANITY

The Book of Common Prayer: A Spiritual Treasure Chest—Selections Annotated & Explained
Annotation by The Rev. Canon C. K. Robertson, PhD; Foreword by The Most Rev. Katharine Jefferts Schori; Preface by Archbishop Desmond Tutu
Makes available the riches of this spiritual treasure chest for all who are interested in deepening their life of prayer, building stronger relationships and making a difference in their world. 5½ x 8½, 208 pp, Quality PB, 978-1-59473-524-0 **$16.99**

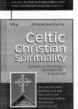

Celtic Christian Spirituality: Essential Writings—Annotated & Explained
Annotation by Mary C. Earle; Foreword by John Philip Newell
Explores how the writings of this lively tradition embody the gospel.
5½ x 8½, 176 pp, Quality PB, 978-1-59473-302-4 **$16.99**

Desert Fathers and Mothers: Early Christian Wisdom Sayings—Annotated & Explained *Annotation by Christine Valters Paintner, PhD*
Opens up wisdom of the desert fathers and mothers for readers with no previous knowledge of Western monasticism and early Christianity.
5½ x 8½, 192 pp, Quality PB, 978-1-59473-373-4 **$16.99**

The End of Days: Essential Selections from Apocalyptic Texts—Annotated & Explained *Annotation by Robert G. Clouse, PhD*
Helps you understand the complex Christian visions of the end of the world.
5½ x 8½, 224 pp, Quality PB, 978-1-59473-170-9 **$16.99**

The Hidden Gospel of Matthew: Annotated & Explained
Translation & Annotation by Ron Miller
Discover the words and events that have the strongest connection to the historical Jesus.
5½ x 8½, 272 pp, Quality PB, 978-1-59473-038-2 **$16.99**

The Imitation of Christ: Selections Annotated & Explained
Annotation by Paul Wesley Chilcote, PhD; By Thomas à Kempis
Adapted from John Wesley's The Christian's Pattern
Let Jesus's example of holiness, humility and purity of heart be a companion on your own spiritual journey.
5½ x 8½, 224 pp, Quality PB, 978-1-59473-434-2 **$16.99**

The Infancy Gospels of Jesus: Apocryphal Tales from the Childhoods of Mary and Jesus—Annotated & Explained
Translation & Annotation by Stevan Davies; Foreword by A. Edward Siecienski, PhD
A startling presentation of the early lives of Mary, Jesus and other biblical figures that will amuse and surprise you. 5½ x 8½, 176 pp, Quality PB, 978-1-59473-258-4 **$16.99**

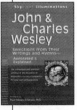

John & Charles Wesley: Selections from Their Writings and Hymns—Annotated & Explained *Annotation by Paul W. Chilcote, PhD*
A unique presentation of the writings of these two inspiring brothers brings together some of the most essential material from their large corpus of work.
5½ x 8½, 288 pp, Quality PB, 978-1-59473-309-3 **$16.99**

Julian of Norwich: Selections from *Revelations of Divine Love*—Annotated & Explained *Annotation by Mary C. Earle; Foreword by Roberta C. Bondi*
Addresses topics including the infinite nature of God, the life of prayer, God's suffering with us, the eternal and undying life of the soul, the motherhood of Jesus and the motherhood of God and more.
5½ x 8½, 224 pp, Quality PB, 978-1-59473-513-4 **$16.99**

Sacred Texts—continued

CHRISTIANITY—continued

The Lost Sayings of Jesus: Teachings from Ancient Christian, Jewish, Gnostic and Islamic Sources—Annotated & Explained
Translation & Annotation by Andrew Phillip Smith; Foreword by Stephan A. Hoeller
Depicts Jesus as a Wisdom teacher who speaks to people of all faiths as a mystic and spiritual master. 5½ x 8½, 240 pp, Quality PB, 978-1-59473-172-3 **$16.99**

Philokalia: The Eastern Christian Spiritual Texts—Selections
Annotated & Explained *Annotation by Allyne Smith; Translation by G. E. H. Palmer, Phillip Sherrard and Bishop Kallistos Ware* The first approachable introduction to the wisdom of the Philokalia. 5½ x 8½, 240 pp, Quality PB, 978-1-59473-103-7 **$18.99**

The Sacred Writings of Paul: Selections Annotated & Explained
Translation & Annotation by Ron Miller Leads you into the exciting immediacy of Paul's teachings. 5½ x 8½, 224 pp, Quality PB, 978-1-59473-213-3 **$16.99**

Saint Augustine of Hippo: Selections from *Confessions* and Other Essential Writings—Annotated & Explained
Annotation by Joseph T. Kelley, PhD; Translation by the Augustinian Heritage Institute
Provides insight into the mind and heart of this foundational Christian figure.
5½ x 8½, 272 pp, Quality PB, 978-1-59473-282-9 **$18.99**

Saint Ignatius Loyola—The Spiritual Writings: Selections
Annotated & Explained *Annotation by Mark Mossa, SJ* Focuses on the practical mysticism of Ignatius of Loyola. 5½ x 8½, 288 pp, Quality PB, 978-1-59473-301-7 **$18.99**

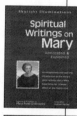

Sex Texts from the Bible: Selections Annotated & Explained
Translation & Annotation by Teresa J. Hornsby; Foreword by Amy-Jill Levine
Demystifies the Bible's ideas on gender roles, marriage, sexual orientation, virginity, lust and sexual pleasure. 5½ x 8½, 208 pp, Quality PB, 978-1-59473-217-1 **$16.99**

Spiritual Writings on Mary: Annotated & Explained
Annotation by Mary Ford-Grabowsky; Foreword by Andrew Harvey
Examines the role of Mary, the mother of Jesus, as a source of inspiration in history and in life today. 5½ x 8½, 272 pp, Quality PB, 978-1-59473-001-6 **$16.99**

The Way of a Pilgrim: The Jesus Prayer Journey—Annotated & Explained
Translation & Annotation by Gleb Pokrovsky; Foreword by Andrew Harvey A classic of Russian Orthodox spirituality. 5½ x 8½, 160 pp, Illus., Quality PB, 978-1-893361-31-7 **$15.99**

GNOSTICISM

Gnostic Writings on the Soul: Annotated & Explained
Translation & Annotation by Andrew Phillip Smith; Foreword by Stephan A. Hoeller
Reveals the inspiring ways your soul can remember and return to its unique, divine purpose. 5½ x 8½, 144 pp, Quality PB, 978-1-59473-220-1 **$16.99**

The Gospel of Philip: Annotated & Explained
Translation & Annotation by Andrew Phillip Smith; Foreword by Stevan Davies
Reveals otherwise unrecorded sayings of Jesus and fragments of Gnostic mythology.
5½ x 8½, 160 pp, Quality PB, 978-1-59473-111-2 **$16.99**

The Gospel of Thomas: Annotated & Explained
Translation & Annotation by Stevan Davies; Foreword by Andrew Harvey
Sheds new light on the origins of Christianity and portrays Jesus as a wisdom-loving sage.
5½ x 8½, 192 pp, Quality PB, 978-1-893361-45-4 **$16.99**

The Secret Book of John: The Gnostic Gospel—Annotated & Explained
Translation & Annotation by Stevan Davies The most significant and influential text of the ancient Gnostic religion. 5½ x 8½, 208 pp, Quality PB, 978-1-59473-082-5 **$18.99**

See Inspiration for *Perennial Wisdom for the Spiritually Independent: Sacred Teachings—Annotated & Explained*

Sacred Texts—continued

JUDAISM

The Book of Job: Annotated & Explained
Translation and Annotation by Donald Kraus; Foreword by Dr. Marc Brettler
Clarifies for today's readers what Job is, how to overcome difficulties in the text, and what it may mean for us. 5½ x 8½, 256 pp, Quality PB, 978-1-59473-389-5 **$16.99**

The Divine Feminine in Biblical Wisdom Literature
Selections Annotated & Explained
Translation & Annotation by Rabbi Rami Shapiro; Foreword by Rev. Cynthia Bourgeault, PhD
Uses the Hebrew Bible and Wisdom literature to explain Sophia's way of wisdom and illustrate Her creative energy. 5½ x 8½, 240 pp, Quality PB, 978-1-59473-109-9 **$18.99**

Ecclesiastes: Annotated & Explained
Translation & Annotation by Rabbi Rami Shapiro; Foreword by Rev. Barbara Cawthorne Crafton
A timeless teaching on living well amid uncertainty and insecurity.
5½ x 8½, 160 pp, Quality PB, 978-1-59473-287-4 **$16.99**

Embracing the Divine Feminine: Finding God through the Ecstasy of Physical Love—The Song of Songs Annotated & Explained
Translation & Annotation by Rabbi Rami Shapiro; Foreword by Rev. Cynthia Bourgeault, PhD
Restores the Song of Songs' eroticism and interprets it as a celebration of the love between the Divine Feminine and the contemporary spiritual seeker.
5½ x 8½, 176 pp, Quality PB, 978-1-59473-575-2 **$16.99**

Ethics of the Sages: Pirke Avot—Annotated & Explained
Translation & Annotation by Rabbi Rami Shapiro Clarifies the ethical teachings of the early Rabbis. 5½ x 8½, 192 pp, Quality PB, 978-1-59473-207-2 **$16.99**

Hasidic Tales: Annotated & Explained
Translation & Annotation by Rabbi Rami Shapiro; Foreword by Andrew Harvey
Introduces the legendary tales of the impassioned Hasidic rabbis, presenting them as stories rather than as parables. 5½ x 8½, 240 pp, Quality PB, 978-1-893361-86-7 **$18.99**

The Hebrew Prophets: Selections Annotated & Explained
Translation & Annotation by Rabbi Rami Shapiro; Foreword by Rabbi Zalman M. Schachter-Shalomi (z"l)
Makes the wisdom of these timeless teachers available to readers with no previous knowledge of the prophets. 5½ x 8½, 224 pp, Quality PB, 978-1-59473-037-5 **$16.99**

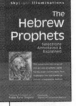

Maimonides—Essential Teachings on Jewish Faith & Ethics
The Book of Knowledge & the Thirteen Principles of Faith—Annotated & Explained
Translation and Annotation by Rabbi Marc D. Angel, PhD
Opens up for us Maimonides's views on the nature of God, providence, prophecy, free will, human nature, repentance and more.
5½ x 8½, 224 pp, Quality PB, 978-1-59473-311-6 **$18.99**

Proverbs: Annotated & Explained
Translation and Annotation by Rabbi Rami Shapiro
Demonstrates how these complex poetic forms are actually straightforward instructions to live simply, without rationalizations and excuses.
5½ x 8½, 288 pp, Quality PB, 978-1-59473-310-9 **$16.99**

Tanya, the Masterpiece of Hasidic Wisdom
Selections Annotated & Explained *Translation & Annotation by Rabbi Rami Shapiro*
Foreword by Rabbi Zalman M. Schachter-Shalomi (z"l)
Clarifies one of the most powerful and potentially transformative books of Jewish wisdom. 5½ x 8½, 240 pp, Quality PB, 978-1-59473-275-1 **$18.99**

Zohar: Annotated & Explained
Translation & Annotation by Daniel C. Matt; Foreword by Andrew Harvey
The canonical text of Jewish mystical tradition.
5½ x 8½, 176 pp, Quality PB, 978-1-893361-51-5 **$18.99**

See Inspiration for *Perennial Wisdom for the Spiritually Independent: Sacred Teachings—Annotated & Explained*

Sacred Texts—continued

ISLAM

Ghazali on the Principles of Islamic Spirituality
Selections from *The Forty Foundations of Religion*—Annotated & Explained
Translation & Annotation by Aaron Spevack, PhD; Foreword by M. Fethullah Gülen
Makes the core message of this influential spiritual master relevant to anyone seeking a balanced understanding of Islam.
5½ x 8½, 336 pp, Quality PB, 978-1-59473-284-3 **$18.99**

The Qur'an and Sayings of Prophet Muhammad
Selections Annotated & Explained
Annotation by Sohaib N. Sultan; Translation by Yusuf Ali, Revised by Sohaib N. Sultan
Foreword by Jane I. Smith
Presents the foundational wisdom of Islam in an easy-to-use format.
5½ x 8½, 256 pp, Quality PB, 978-1-59473-222-5 **$16.99**

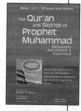

Rumi and Islam: Selections from His Stories, Poems, and Discourses—
Annotated & Explained *Translation & Annotation by Ibrahim Gamard*
Focuses on Rumi's place within the Sufi tradition of Islam, providing insight into the mystical side of the religion. 5½ x 8½, 240 pp, Quality PB, 978-1-59473-002-3 **$18.99**

See Inspiration for *Perennial Wisdom for the Spiritually Independent: Sacred Teachings—Annotated & Explained*

EASTERN RELIGIONS

The Art of War—Spirituality for Conflict: Annotated & Explained
By Sun Tzu; Annotation by Thomas Huynh; Translation by Thomas Huynh and the Editors at Sonshi.com; Foreword by Marc Benioff; Preface by Thomas Cleary
Highlights principles that encourage a perceptive and spiritual approach to conflict.
5½ x 8½, 256 pp, Quality PB, 978-1-59473-244-7 **$16.99**

Bhagavad Gita: Annotated & Explained
Translation by Shri Purohit Swami; Annotation by Kendra Crossen Burroughs
Foreword by Andrew Harvey Presents the classic text's teachings—with no previous knowledge of Hinduism required. 5½ x 8½, 192 pp, Quality PB, 978-1-893361-28-7 **$18.99**

Chuang-tzu: The Tao of Perfect Happiness—Selections Annotated & Explained
Translation & Annotation by Livia Kohn, PhD
Presents Taoism's central message of reverence for the "Way" of the natural world.
5½ x 8½, 240 pp, Quality PB, 978-1-59473-296-6 **$16.99**

Confucius, the *Analects*: The Path of the Sage—Selections Annotated
& Explained *Annotation by Rodney L. Taylor, PhD; Translation by James Legge,*
Revised by Rodney L. Taylor, PhD Explores the ethical and spiritual meaning behind the Confucian way of learning and self-cultivation.
5½ x 8½, 192 pp, Quality PB, 978-1-59473-306-2 **$16.99**

Dhammapada: Annotated & Explained
Translation by Max Müller, Revised by Jack Maguire; Annotation by Jack Maguire
Foreword by Andrew Harvey Contains all of Buddhism's key teachings, plus commentary that explains all the names, terms and references.
5½ x 8½, 160 pp, b/w photos, Quality PB, 978-1-893361-42-3 **$14.95**

Selections from the Gospel of Sri Ramakrishna: Annotated & Explained
Translation by Swami Nikhilananda; Annotation by Kendra Crossen Burroughs
Foreword by Andrew Harvey Introduces the fascinating world of the Indian mystic and the universal appeal of his message. 5½ x 8½, 240 pp, b/w photos, Quality PB, 978-1-893361-46-1 **$16.95**

Tao Te Ching: Annotated & Explained
Translation & Annotation by Derek Lin; Foreword by Lama Surya Das
Introduces an Eastern classic in an accessible, poetic and completely original way.
5½ x 8½, 208 pp, Quality PB, 978-1-59473-204-1 **$16.99**

Women's Interest

There's a Woman in the Pulpit: Christian Clergywomen Share Their Hard Days, Holy Moments & the Healing Power of Humor
Edited by Rev. Martha Spong; Foreword by Rev. Carol Howard Merritt
Offers insight into the lives of Christian clergywomen and the rigors that come with commitment to religious life, representing fourteen denominations as well as dozens of seminaries and colleges. 6 x 9, 240 pp, Quality PB, 978-1-59473-588-2 **$18.99**

She Lives! Sophia Wisdom Works in the World
By Rev. Jann Aldredge-Clanton, PhD
Fascinating narratives of clergy and laypeople who are changing the institutional church and society by restoring biblical female divine names and images to Christian theology, worship symbolism and liturgical language.
6 x 9, 320 pp, Quality PB, 978-1-59473-573-8 **$18.99**

Birthing God: Women's Experiences of the Divine
By Lana Dalberg; Foreword by Kathe Schaaf
Powerful narratives of suffering, love and hope that inspire both personal and collective transformation. 6 x 9, 304 pp, Quality PB, 978-1-59473-480-9 **$18.99**

Women, Spirituality and Transformative Leadership
Where Grace Meets Power
Edited by Kathe Schaaf, Kay Lindahl, Kathleen S. Hurty, PhD, and Reverend Guo Cheen
A dynamic conversation on the power of women's spiritual leadership and its emerging patterns of transformation.
6 x 9, 288 pp, Quality PB, 978-1-59473-548-6 **$18.99**; HC, 978-1-59473-313-0 **$24.99**

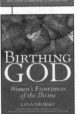

Spiritually Healthy Divorce: Navigating Disruption with Insight & Hope
By Carolyne Call A spiritual map to help you move through the twists and turns of divorce. 6 x 9, 224 pp, Quality PB, 978-1-59473-288-1 **$16.99**

Bread, Body, Spirit: Finding the Sacred in Food
Edited and with Introductions by Alice Peck 6 x 9, 224 pp, Quality PB, 978-1-59473-242-3 **$19.99**

Dance—The Sacred Art: The Joy of Movement as a Spiritual Practice
By Cynthia Winton-Henry 5½ x 8½, 224 pp, Quality PB, 978-1-59473-268-3 **$16.99**

Daughters of the Desert: Stories of Remarkable Women from Christian, Jewish and Muslim Traditions *By Claire Rudolf Murphy, Meghan Nuttall Sayres, Mary Cronk Farrell, Sarah Conover and Betsy Wharton*
5½ x 8½, 192 pp, Illus., Quality PB, 978-1-59473-106-8 **$18.99** Inc. reader's discussion guide

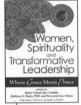

The Divine Feminine in Biblical Wisdom Literature
Selections Annotated & Explained
Translation & Annotation by Rabbi Rami Shapiro; Foreword by Rev. Cynthia Bourgeault, PhD
5½ x 8½, 240 pp, Quality PB, 978-1-59473-109-9 **$18.99**

Divining the Body: Reclaim the Holiness of Your Physical Self
By Jan Phillips 8 x 8, 256 pp, Quality PB, 978-1-59473-080-1 **$18.99**

Honoring Motherhood: Prayers, Ceremonies & Blessings
Edited and with Introductions by Lynn L. Caruso
5 x 7¼, 272 pp, Quality PB, 978-1-58473-384-0 **$9.99**; HC, 978-1-59473-239-3 **$19.99**

New Feminist Christianity: Many Voices, Many Views
Edited by Mary E. Hunt and Diann L. Neu
6 x 9, 384 pp, Quality PB, 978-1-59473-435-9 **$19.99**; HC, 978-1-59473-285-0 **$24.99**

Next to Godliness: Finding the Sacred in Housekeeping
Edited by Alice Peck 6 x 9, 224 pp, Quality PB, 978-1-59473-214-0 **$19.99**

The Triumph of Eve & Other Subversive Bible Tales
By Matt Biers-Ariel 5½ x 8½, 192 pp, Quality PB, 978-1-59473-176-1 **$14.99**

Woman Spirit Awakening in Nature: Growing into the Fullness of Who You Are
By Nancy Barrett Chickerneo, PhD; Foreword by Eileen Fisher
8 x 8, 224 pp, b/w illus., Quality PB, 978-1-59473-250-8 **$16.99**

Women of Color Pray: Voices of Strength, Faith, Healing, Hope and Courage
Edited and with Introductions by Christal M. Jackson 5 x 7¼, 208 pp, Quality PB, 978-1-59473-077-1 **$15.99**

Spirituality

Mere Spirituality
The Spiritual Life According to Henri Nouwen
By Wil Hernandez, PhD, Obl. OSB; Foreword by Ronald Rolheiser

This introduction to Nouwen's spiritual thought distills key insights on the realm of the spiritual life into one concise and compelling overview of his spirituality of the heart.

6 x 9, 160 pp, Quality PB, 978-1-59473-586-8 **$16.99**

The Forgiveness Handbook
Spiritual Wisdom and Practice for the Journey to Freedom, Healing and Peace
Created by the Editors at SkyLight Paths; Introduction by The Rev. Canon Marianne Wells Borg

Offers inspiration, encouragement and spiritual practice from across faith traditions for all who seek hope, wholeness and the freedom that comes from true forgiveness.

6 x 9, 256 pp, Quality PB, 978-1-59473-577-6 **$18.99**

Like a Child
Restoring the Awe, Wonder, Joy and Resiliency of the Human Spirit
By Rev. Timothy J. Mooney

By breaking free from our misperceptions about what it means to be an adult, we can reshape our world and become harbingers of grace. This unique spiritual resource explores Jesus's counsel to become like children in order to enter the kingdom of God. 6 x 9, 160 pp, Quality PB, 978-1-59473-543-1 **$16.99**

The Passionate Jesus: What We Can Learn from Jesus about Love, Fear, Grief, Joy and Living Authentically
By The Rev. Peter Wallace

Reveals Jesus as a passionate figure who was involved, present, connected, honest and direct with others and encourages you to build personal authenticity in every area of your own life. 6 x 9, 208 pp, Quality PB, 978-1-59473-393-2 **$18.99**

Gathering at God's Table: The Meaning of Mission in the Feast of Faith
By Katharine Jefferts Schori

A profound reminder of our role in the larger frame of God's dream for a restored and reconciled world. 6 x 9, 256 pp, HC, 978-1-59473-316-1 **$21.99**

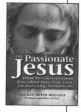

The Heartbeat of God: Finding the Sacred in the Middle of Everything
By Katharine Jefferts Schori; Foreword by Joan Chittister, OSB

Explores our connections to other people, to other nations and with the environment through the lens of faith.

6 x 9, 240 pp, HC, 978-1-59473-292-8 **$21.99**; Quality PB, 978-1-59473-589-9 **$16.99**

Laugh Your Way to Grace: Reclaiming the Spiritual Power of Humor
By Rev. Susan Sparks

A powerful, humorous case for laughter as a spiritual, healing path.

6 x 9, 176 pp, Quality PB, 978-1-59473-280-5 **$16.99**

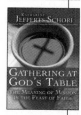

Claiming Earth as Common Ground: The Ecological Crisis through the Lens of Faith
By Andrea Cohen-Kiener; Foreword by Rev. Sally Bingham
6 x 9, 192 pp, Quality PB, 978-1-59473-261-4 **$16.99**

Living into Hope: A Call to Spiritual Action for Such a Time as This
By Rev. Dr. Joan Brown Campbell; Foreword by Karen Armstrong
6 x 9, 208 pp, Quality PB, 978-1-59473-436-6 **$18.99**; HC, 978-1-59473-283-6 **$21.99**

Renewal in the Wilderness
A Spiritual Guide to Connecting with God in the Natural World
By John Lionberger 6 x 9, 176 pp, b/w photos, Quality PB, 978-1-59473-219-5 **$16.99**

A Walk with Four Spiritual Guides: Krishna, Buddha, Jesus, and Ramakrishna
By Andrew Harvey 5½ x 8½, 192 pp, b/w photos & illus., Quality PB, 978-1-59473-138-9 **$18.99**

Spiritual Practice—The Sacred Art of Living Series

Teaching—The Sacred Art: The Joy of Opening Minds & Hearts
By Rev. Jane E. Vennard Explores the elements that make teaching a sacred art, recognizing it as a call to service rather than a job, and a vocation rather than a profession. 5½ x 8½, 160 pp, Quality PB, 978-1-59473-585-1 **$16.99**

Conversation—The Sacred Art: Practicing Presence in an Age of Distraction
By Diane M. Millis, PhD; Foreword by Rev. Tilden Edwards, PhD
5½ x 8½, 192 pp, Quality PB, 978-1-59473-474-8 **$16.99**

Dance—The Sacred Art: The Joy of Movement as a Spiritual Practice
By Cynthia Winton-Henry 5½ x 8½, 224 pp, Quality PB, 978-1-59473-268-3 **$16.99**

Dreaming—The Sacred Art: Incubating, Navigating & Interpreting Sacred Dreams
for Spiritual & Personal Growth *By Lori Joan Swick, PhD*
5½ x 8½, 224 pp, Quality PB, 978-1-59473-544-8 **$16.99**

Fly-Fishing—The Sacred Art: Casting a Fly as a Spiritual Practice
*By Rabbi Eric Eisenkramer and Rev. Michael Attas, MD; Foreword by Chris Wood, CEO,
Trout Unlimited; Preface by Lori Simon, executive director, Casting for Recovery*
5½ x 8½, 160 pp, Quality PB, 978-1-59473-299-7 **$16.99**

Giving—The Sacred Art: Creating a Lifestyle of Generosity
By Lauren Tyler Wright 5½ x 8½, 208 pp, Quality PB, 978-1-59473-224-9 **$16.99**

Haiku—The Sacred Art: A Spiritual Practice in Three Lines
By Margaret D. McGee 5½ x 8½, 192 pp, Quality PB, 978-1-59473-269-0 **$16.99**

Hospitality—The Sacred Art: Discovering the Hidden Spiritual Power of Invitation
and Welcome *By Rev. Nanette Sawyer; Foreword by Rev. Dirk Ficca*
5½ x 8½, 208 pp, Quality PB, 978-1-59473-228-7 **$16.99**

Labyrinths from the Outside In, 2nd Edition
Walking to Spiritual Insight—A Beginner's Guide *By Rev. Dr. Donna Schaper and
Rev. Dr. Carole Ann Camp* 6 x 9, 208 pp, b/w illus. and photos, Quality PB, 978-1-59473-486-1 **$16.99**

Lectio Divina—**The Sacred Art**
Transforming Words & Images into Heart-Centered Prayer
By Christine Valters Paintner, PhD 5½ x 8½, 240 pp, Quality PB, 978-1-59473-300-0 **$16.99**

Pilgrimage—The Sacred Art: Journey to the Center of the Heart
By Dr. Sheryl A. Kujawa-Holbrook 5½ x 8½, 240 pp, Quality PB, 978-1-59473-472-4 **$16.99**

Practicing the Sacred Art of Listening
A Guide to Enrich Your Relationships and Kindle Your Spiritual Life
By Kay Lindahl 8 x 8, 176 pp, Quality PB, 978-1-893361-85-0 **$18.99**

Recovery—The Sacred Art: The Twelve Steps as Spiritual Practice *By Rami Shapiro*
Foreword by Joan Borysenko, PhD 5½ x 8½, 240 pp, Quality PB, 978-1-59473-259-1 **$16.99**

Running—The Sacred Art: Preparing to Practice *By Dr. Warren A. Kay*
Foreword by Kristin Armstrong 5½ x 8½, 160 pp, Quality PB, 978-1-59473-227-0 **$16.99**

The Sacred Art of Chant: Preparing to Practice
By Ana Hernández 5½ x 8½, 192 pp, Quality PB, 978-1-59473-036-8 **$16.99**

The Sacred Art of Fasting: Preparing to Practice
By Thomas Ryan, CSP 5½ x 8½, 192 pp, Quality PB, 978-1-59473-078-8 **$15.99**

The Sacred Art of Forgiveness: Forgiving Ourselves and Others through God's Grace
By Marcia Ford 8 x 8, 176 pp, Quality PB, 978-1-59473-175-4 **$18.99**

The Sacred Art of Listening: Forty Reflections for Cultivating a Spiritual Practice
By Kay Lindahl; Illus. by Amy Schnapper 8 x 8, 160 pp, b/w illus., Quality PB, 978-1-893361-44-7 **$16.99**

The Sacred Art of Lovingkindness: Preparing to Practice
By Rabbi Rami Shapiro; Foreword by Marcia Ford 5½ x 8½, 176 pp, Quality PB, 978-1-59473-151-8 **$16.99**

Spiritual Adventures in the Snow: Skiing & Snowboarding as Renewal for Your Soul
By Dr. Marcia McFee and Rev. Karen Foster; Foreword by Paul Arthur
5½ x 8½, 208 pp, Quality PB, 978-1-59473-270-6 **$16.99**

Thanking & Blessing—The Sacred Art: Spiritual Vitality through Gratefulness
By Jay Marshall, PhD; Foreword by Philip Gulley 5½ x 8½, 176 pp, Quality PB, 978-1-59473-231-7 **$16.99**

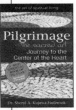

Writing—The Sacred Art: Beyond the Page to Spiritual Practice
By Rami Shapiro and Aaron Shapiro 5½ x 8½, 192 pp, Quality PB, 978-1-59473-372-7 **$16.99**

Prayer / Meditation

The Advent of God's Word
Listening for the Power of the Divine Whisper—A Daily Retreat &
Devotional *By Rev. Dr. Brenda K. Buckwell, Obl. OSB*
For those who find themselves struggling with no time for prayer during the busy
Advent season. Step-by-step creative exercises help you celebrate the birth of Jesus.
6 x 9, 208 pp, Quality PB, 978-1-59473-576-9 **$16.99**

Calling on God
Inclusive Christian Prayers for Three Years of Sundays
By Peter Bankson and Deborah Sokolove
Prayers for today's world, vividly written for Christians who long for a way to
talk to and about God that feels fresh yet still connected to tradition.
6 x 9, 400 pp, Quality PB, 978-1-59473-568-4 **$18.99**

The Worship Leader's Guide to Calling on God
8½ x 11, 20 pp, PB, 978-1-59473-591-2 **$9.99**

Openings, 2nd Edition
A Daybook of Saints, Sages, Psalms and Prayer Practices
By Rev. Larry J. Peacock
For anyone hungry for a richer prayer life, this prayer book offers daily inspiration to help you move closer to God. Draws on a wide variety of resources—lives
of saints and sages from every age, psalms, and suggestions for personal reflection
and practice. 6 x 9, 448 pp, Quality PB, 978-1-59473-545-5 **$18.99**

**Openings: A Daybook of Saints, Sages, Psalms and
Prayer Practices—Leader's Guide** 8½ x 11, 12 pp, PB, 978-1-59473-572-1 **$9.99**

Honest to God Prayer: Spirituality as Awareness, Empowerment,
Relinquishment and Paradox *By Kent Ira Groff*
6 x 9, 192 pp, Quality PB, 978-1-59473-433-5 **$16.99**

Lectio Divina—**The Sacred Art**
Transforming Words & Images into Heart-Centered Prayer
By Christine Valters Paintner, PhD 5½ x 8½, 240 pp, Quality PB, 978-1-59473-300-0 **$16.99**

Men Pray: Voices of Strength, Faith, Healing, Hope and Courage
Created by the Editors at SkyLight Paths; With Introductions by Brian D. McLaren
5 x 7¼, 192 pp, HC, 978-1-59473-395-6 **$16.99**

Secrets of Prayer: A Multifaith Guide to Creating Personal Prayer in Your Life
By Nancy Corcoran, CSJ 6 x 9, 160 pp, Quality PB, 978-1-59473-215-7 **$16.99**

Women of Color Pray: Voices of Strength, Faith, Healing, Hope and Courage
Edited and with Introductions by Christal M. Jackson
5 x 7¼, 208 pp, Quality PB, 978-1-59473-077-1 **$15.99**

Prayer / M. Basil Pennington, OCSO

Finding Grace at the Center, 3rd Edition: The Beginning of
Centering Prayer *With Thomas Keating, OCSO, and Thomas E. Clarke, SJ*
Foreword by Rev. Cynthia Bourgeault, PhD A practical guide to a simple and beautiful
form of meditative prayer. 5 x 7¼, 128 pp, Quality PB, 978-1-59473-182-2 **$12.99**

The Monks of Mount Athos: A Western Monk's Extraordinary
Spiritual Journey on Eastern Holy Ground *Foreword by Archimandrite Dionysios*
Explores the landscape, monastic communities and food of Athos.
6 x 9, 352 pp, Quality PB, 978-1-893361-78-2 **$18.95**

Psalms: A Spiritual Commentary *Illus. by Phillip Ratner*
Reflections on some of the most beloved passages from the Bible's most widely
read book. 6 x 9, 176 pp, 24 full-page b/w illus., Quality PB, 978-1-59473-234-8 **$16.99**

The Song of Songs: A Spiritual Commentary *Illus. by Phillip Ratner*
Explore the Bible's most challenging mystical text.
6 x 9, 160 pp, 14 full-page b/w illus., Quality PB, 978-1-59473-235-5 **$16.99**
HC, 978-1-59473-004-7 **$19.99**

About SKYLIGHT PATHS Publishing

SkyLight Paths Publishing is creating a place where people of different spiritual traditions come together for challenge and inspiration, a place where we can help each other understand the mystery that lies at the heart of our existence.

Through spirituality, our religious beliefs are increasingly becoming a part of our lives—rather than *apart* from our lives. While many of us may be more interested than ever in spiritual growth, we may be less firmly planted in traditional religion. Yet, we do want to deepen our relationship to the sacred, to learn from our own as well as from other faith traditions, and to practice in new ways.

SkyLight Paths sees both believers and seekers as a community that increasingly transcends traditional boundaries of religion and denomination—people wanting to learn from each other, *walking together, finding the way.*

For your information and convenience, at the back of this book we have provided a list of other SkyLight Paths books you might find interesting and useful. They cover the following subjects:

Buddhism / Zen	Gnosticism	Poetry
Catholicism	Hinduism / Vedanta	Prayer
Chaplaincy		Religious Etiquette
Children's Books	Inspiration	Retirement & Later-Life Spirituality
Christianity	Islam / Sufism	
Comparative Religion	Judaism	Spiritual Biography
	Meditation	Spiritual Direction
Earth-Based Spirituality	Mindfulness	Spirituality
	Monasticism	Women's Interest
Enneagram	Mysticism	Worship
Global Spiritual Perspectives	Personal Growth	

Or phone, fax, mail or email to: SKYLIGHT PATHS Publishing
Sunset Farm Offices, Route 4 • P.O. Box 237 • Woodstock, Vermont 05091
Tel: (802) 457-4000 • Fax: (802) 457-4004 • www.skylightpaths.com
Credit card orders: **(800) 962-4544** (8:30AM–5:30PM EST Monday–Friday)
Generous discounts on quantity orders. SATISFACTION GUARANTEED. Prices subject to change.

For more information about each book, visit our website at www.skylightpaths.com.